Coleção
Eu gosto m@is

ENSINO FUNDAMENTAL

INGLÊS

Edgar Laporta

6º ano

1ª EDIÇÃO
SÃO PAULO
2012

IBEP

Coleção Eu Gosto Mais
Inglês 6º ano
© IBEP, 2012

Diretor superintendente	Jorge Yunes
Gerente editorial	Célia de Assis
Editor	Angelo Gabriel Rozner
Assistente editorial	Fernanda dos Santos Silva
Revisão técnica	Mariett Regina R. de Azevedo
Revisão	Rachel Prochoroff
Coordenadora de arte	Karina Monteiro
Assistente de arte	Marilia Vilela
	Tomás Troppmair
Coordenadora de iconografia	Maria do Céu Pires Passuello
Assistente de iconografia	Adriana Neves
	Wilson de Castilho
Ilustrações	Lie Kobayashi
Produção editorial	Paula Calviello
Produção gráfica	José Antônio Ferraz
Assistente de produção gráfica	Eliane M. M. Ferreira
Projeto gráfico e capa	Departamento de arte IBEP
Editoração eletrônica	Formato Comunicação

CIP-BRASIL. CATALOGAÇÃO-NA-FONTE
SINDICATO NACIONAL DOS EDITORES DE LIVROS, RJ

L32i

Laporta, Edgar
    Inglês : 6º ano / Edgar Laporta. - 1.ed. - São Paulo : IBEP, 2012.
    il. ; 28 cm. (Eu gosto mais)

    ISBN 978-85-342-3444-3 (aluno) - 978-85-342-3448-1 (mestre)

    1. Língua inglesa - Estudo e ensino (Ensino fundamental). I. Título. II. Série.

12-6210   CDD: 372.6521
                                                            CDU: 373.3.016=111

28.08.12   05.09.12   038544

1ª edição - São Paulo - 2012
Todos os direitos reservados

IBEP

Av. Alexandre Mackenzie, 619 - Jaguaré
São Paulo - SP - 05322-000 - Brasil - Tel.: (11) 2799-7799
www.editoraibep.com.br   editoras@ibep-nacional.com.br

Impressão Serzegraf - Setembro 2016

Apresentação

O inglês é um idioma de grande importância no mundo globalizado de hoje. Está presente em nossa vida diária, na TV, no cinema, na Internet, nas músicas, nos livros, nas revistas etc.

Há muito tempo, tornou-se um dos principais meios de comunicação no turismo, no comércio mundial, nas competições esportivas, nos congressos sobre ciência e tecnologia, nos meios diplomáticos, nos encontros de líderes mundiais etc. Por isso, cada vez mais pessoas estudam e falam inglês.

Com o objetivo de despertar em você o gosto pelo idioma inglês, tivemos a preocupação de abordar textos variados e que se relacionam com sua vida.

As atividades de interpretação dos textos levam você a ler e reler o texto para encontrar as respostas adequadas às perguntas.

Sempre que você tiver alguma dificuldade em descobrir o sentido de palavras ou expressões do texto, lembre-se de que há no final do livro o vocabulário geral para ajudá-lo.

As noções de gramática são apresentadas na seção *Learn this* de forma simples e abreviada. Logo a seguir, você vai treiná-las com exercícios rápidos e simples.

Participe ativamente das aulas e aproveite esta oportunidade para aprender inglês.

O autor

Sumário

Lesson 1 – Greetings; personal pronouns; interrogative expressions 7

Dialogue: *Meeting a friend* 7
- Learn this 8
- Activities 9
- Listen and write – dictation 11
- Fun time 11
- Role-play – oral drill 12
- Let's sing 12

Lesson 2 – Introducing yourself; indefinite articles; interrogative pronouns 13

Dialogue: *What's your name?* 13
- Learn this 14
- Activities 14
- Role-play – oral drill 16

Lesson 3 – Interrogative form of verb to be; adjectives 17

Dialogue: *An interview* 17
- Text comprehension 18
- Activities 19
- Listen and write – dictation 21
- Fun time 21
- Let's sing 23
- Role-play – oral drill 23

Lesson 4 – Definite article; verb can; verb to be 24

Dialogue: *Can I see this photo?* 24
- Text comprehension 25

- Learn this 25
- Activities 26
- Listen and write – dictation 29
- Fun time 30
- Review 30

Lesson 5 – Negative form of verb to be; opposite of adjectives 32

Dialogue: *Guess who! A gessing game* 32
- Text comprehension 33
- Learn this 33
- Activities 34
- Fun time 36
- Role-play – oral drill 37

Lesson 6 – Negative form of verb to be and verb can 38

Dialogue: *I'm not well, mom* 38
- Text comprehension 39
- Learn this 39
- Activities 40
- Listen and write – dictation 41
- Fun time 41
- Review 41
- Role-play – oral drill 43

Lesson 7 – Demonstrative pronouns: this, that 44

Dialogue: *A strange plumber* 44
- Text comprehension 45
- Learn this 45

| Activities | 46 |
| Let's sing | 47 |

Lesson 8 – Demonstrative adjectives: these, those ... 48

Dialogue: *Visiting Rio de Janeiro*	48
Text comprehension	49
Learn this	50
Activities	51
Listen and write – dictation	52
Fun time	53

Lesson 9 – Prepositions: in, on, under; interrogative word where ... 54

Dialogue: *Where's my cell phone?*	54
Text comprehension	56
Learn this	56

Text: *A hungry cat*	57
Text comprehension	57
Activities	58

Lesson 10 – Cardinal numbers; clothes; colors ... 60

Dialogue: *In a shop*	60
Text comprehension	62
Numbers	63
Add, subtration, multiplication, division	64
Listen and write – dictation	67
Fun time	67
Let's sing	67
Review	68

Lesson 11 – Affirmative and interrogative forms of verb there to be ... 69

Text: *On a farm*	69
Learn this	70
Activities	70
Fun time	71
Role-play – oral-drill	71

| Text: *A thrilling poem* | 71 |

Lesson 12 – Affirmative and negative forms of verb can ... 72

Dialogue: *A bird and a nest*	72
Text comprehension	73
Learn this	73
Activities	74
Role-play – oral-drill	76
Text comprehension	76
Review	77

Lesson 13 – How old are you? ... 78

Dialogue: *How old are you?*	78
Text comprehension	79
Learn this	79
Activities	79
Role-play – oral-drill	80

Lesson 14 – Genitive case ... 81

Text: *John's family*	81
Text comprehension	82
Learn this	83

| Activities 84
| Fun time 86
| Role-play – oral drill 87
| Dialogue: *Betty's house* 87

Lesson 15 – Colors 89
Text: *A picture in many colors* 89
| Text comprehension 90
| Activities 90
| Fun time 92
| Role-play – oral drill 93

Lesson 16 – Possessive adjectives: his, her, their 94
Dialogue 1: *A guessing game* 94
Dialogue 2: *What color is her hair? What color are her eyes?* 95
| Text comprehension 96
| Learn this 96
| Activities 97
| Review 97

Lesson 17 – Verbs go, do, watch; prepositions of time 99
Text: *Jessica's daily routine* 99
| Text comprehension 101
| Learn this 102
| Activities 102

Capítulo 18 – Telling the time, days of the week 103
Dialogue: *What's the time?* 103
| Text comprehension 104

Dialogue: *Alice's party* 104
| Text comprehension 104
| Learn this 105
| Activities 106
| Role-play – oral drill 107

Lesson 19 – Simple present of verb to have 108
Text: *A penpal* 108
| Text comprehension 109
| Learn this 109
| Let's sing 110

Additional texts 111
Text: *Water* 111
| Text comprehension 112
| Activities 113
| Listen and write – dictation 114
| Text comprehension 114
Text: *At the zoo* 114
| Text comprehension 114
Text: *My school* 115
| Text comprehension 115
Text: *Silvia introduces her family* 116
| Text comprehension 117
Dialogue: *The blind man and the guide* 117

General vocabulary 118

Lesson 1

GREETINGS;
PERSONAL PRONOUNS;
INTERROGATIVE EXPRESSIONS

Meeting a friend

Jessica: Good morning, Marcel.
Marcel: Good morning, Jessica.
Jessica: How are you?
Marcel: I'm fine, thanks, and you?
Jessica: I'm well, thanks.
Marcel: Any news?
Jessica: No news.
Marcel: So long, Jessica. See you tomorrow.
Jessica: Bye! See you tomorrow at school.

LEARN THIS

1. Personal pronouns

PERSONAL PRONOUNS	
1ª pessoa do singular	**I** (eu)
2ª pessoa do singular	**You** (tu, você)
3ª pessoa do singular masculina	**He** (ele)
3ª pessoa do singular feminina	**She** (ela)
3ª pessoa do singular neutra	**It** (refere-se a animais ou coisas)
1ª pessoa do plural	**We** (nós)
2ª pessoa do plural	**You** (vós, vocês)
3ª pessoa do plural	**They** (eles, elas, coisas e animais)

2. Greetings

(Usa-se **good morning** ao cumprimentar desde o nascer do Sol até o meio-dia).

Usa-se **good evening** ao encontrar uma pessoa à noite ou à tardinha.

Usa-se **good night** ao despedir-se de alguém à noite. Saudação comum entre amigos:

Nice to meet you.
Glad to meet you. } Prazer em conhecê-lo(a).
Pleased to meet you.

Nice to meet you, too. } Prazer em conhecê-lo(a), também.

Word bank
Good morning: bom dia
Good afternoon: boa tarde.
Good evening: boa noite.
Good night: boa noite.
So long: até logo.
Good-bye (bye-bye): até logo, adeus.
Welcome: bem-vindo.
See you tomorrow: até amanhã.
See you later: até mais tarde.
Hi, hello: oi! olá!

Observações

1. **How are you?** (Como vai você?)
2. **I am fine, thanks.** (Eu estou bem, obrigado.)
   I am well. (Estou bem.)
3. **I'm** é a forma abreviada de **I am** (eu sou/eu estou).
4. **What's** é a forma abreviada de **What is**.
   Exemplo: **What's your name?** (Qual é o seu nome?)

ACTIVITIES

1 Write the greetings according to the positions of the Sun and the Moon:

_____   _____   _____

2 What are the greetings that begin with the word good?

_____

3 Rewrite the dialogue substituting the underlined expression for another. Answer in your copybook.

Jessica: Good <u>morning</u>, Marcel.

Marcel: Good <u>morning</u>, Jessica.

Jessica: How are you?

Marcel: I'm <u>fine</u>, thanks, and you?

Jessica: I'm <u>well</u>, thanks.

Marcel: Any news?

Jessica: No news.

Marcel: <u>So long</u>, Jessica. See you tomorrow.

Jessica: Bye! See you tomorrow at <u>school</u>.

> **Word bank**
>
> **a.m.:** ante meridian (antes do meio-dia)
> **p.m.:** post meridian (depois do meio-dia)
> **any:** algum(a)
> **no:** nenhum(a)
> **tomorrow:** amanhã
> **park:** parque
> **club:** clube
> **school:** escola

4 Write a dialogue in English according to the instructions below. Use your copybook:

a) Comece dizendo "Bom dia" à pessoa e perguntando: "Qual é seu nome?"

b) Ela vai responder: "Eu sou a secretária. Meu nome é Maria."

c) Você continua o diálogo dizendo: "E eu sou estudante. Meu nome é Carlos."

d) Ela responde: "Olá, Carlos! Prazer em conhecê-lo."

5 Translate into English:

Dialogue 1

Jim: Bom dia, Maria. Como vai você?
_____

Maria: Eu estou bem. E você?
_____

Jim: Eu estou bem também.
_____

Dialogue 2

Teacher: Qual é o seu nome?
_____

Sara: Meu nome é Sara.
_____

Sara: Até logo, professor!
_____

Teacher: Até amanhã, Sara.
_____

6 Explain in Portuguese the difference between good evening and good night.
_____
_____

7 Complete the dialogue:

Hello! What's your name?
_____

How are you?
_____

I am an office-boy. And you?
_____

Nice to meet you!
_____

> **Word bank**
> **fine:** ótimo(a)
> **well:** bem
> **not well:** indisposto
> **ill:** doente
> **happy:** feliz
> **unhappy:** infeliz, descontente

10 teen

8 Look at the pictures and fill in the balloons with a dialogue:

LISTEN AND WRITE – DICTATION

Good _____.
Good morning, _____.
_____ are _____?
_____, thanks. And _____?
_____ well. So _____.
So _____.

FUN TIME

1. Tarde
2. Boa noite (despedindo-se)
3. Boa noite
4. Bem-vindo
5. Manhã
6. Alô, olá

2 Draw the Sun or the Moon according to the greetings:

Good morning.	Good afternoon.	Good evening.	Good night.

ROLE-PLAY – ORAL DRILL

1 Agora você vai cumprimentar seus colegas em inglês. Passe entre as carteiras comprimentando-os com **"Hi!"** e pergunte seus nomes, usando a pergunta **"What's your name?"** Eles devem responder em inglês **"I am"** ou **"My name is..."** A seguir, você agradece com a expressão: **"Thank you."**

2 Que tal encenar o diálogo inicial da lição? Uma aluna faz o papel da Jéssica e um aluno o de Marcel. Usem os próprios nomes. Vocês podem usar outras expressões como **Hi** ou **Hello** no começo do diálogo, e **So long** ou **See you later** na despedida.

LET'S SING

I am a cowboy

I am a cowboy.
I begin my work in the morning:
Good morning, flowers!
Good morning, sun!
Good morning…

I come back home,
Happy in the evening:
Good evening, birds!
Good evening, sky!
Good evening…

It's time to sleep.
Oh! Oh! It's night.
Good night, my son!
Good night, my wife!
Good night, my love!

Antes de cantar a música, ouça atentamente o professor ou o CD. Preste atenção na pronúncia das palavras.

Lesson 2

INTRODUCING YOURSELF:
INDEFINITE ARTICLES
INTERROGATIVE PRONOUNS

Word bank

hi: oi (informal)
surname (England): sobrenome
last name (USA): sobrenome
nice: bacana
too: também

What's your name?

Panel 1:
— Hi!
— Hi!

Panel 2:
— My name is Wilson. What's your name?
— My name is Jane Oliveira. And you? What's your surname?

Panel 3:
— My surname is Santos. I am Wilson Santos. Jane, you are a nice girl. I like you.
— Thank you, Wilson. You are nice, too.

Panel 4:
— Jane, who is your teacher?
— My teacher is Rose.

Panel 5:
— Oh! Rose is my teacher, too. Then we are in the same class

Panel 6:
— See you tomorrow!
— So long!

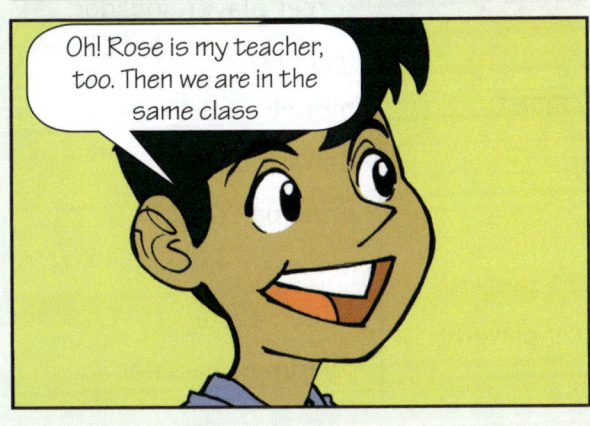

LEARN THIS

1. **Personal pronoun I** (pronome pessoal eu):
   I significa eu e se escreve sempre com maiúscula.
2. **Interrogative pronoun** (pronomes interrogativos):
   What significa o quê, qual.
   Ex.: **What's your occupation?** (Qual é sua profissão?). Podemos abreviar **what is** por **what's**.
3. **Who** é pronome interrogativo que se refere sempre a pessoas.
   Ex.: – **Who is she?** (Quem é ela?.) – **She is my teacher**. (Ela é minha professora.)
   Who are you? frase interrogativa que significa Quem é você?
   Podemos abreviar **who is** por **who's**.
4. **Indefinite articles** (artigos indefinidos): **a, an**
   - **a** significa um, uma e é usado diante de palavras que começam com som de consoante.
     Exemplos: **a student – a pilot – a singer – a lamp**.
   - **an** significa um, uma e é usado diante de palavras que começam com som de vogal
     (ou **h** mudo). Exemplos: **an artist – an orange – an hour**.
     A e **an** são formas usadas no singular. Em inglês, não se usa artigo indefinido no plural.
     Exemplo: **a boy – boys**.

ACTIVITIES

1 Observe the model and do the same:

a) **Who's he?**
   He's Felipe Massa.
   What's he? (a Brazilian car racer)
   He's a Brazilian car racer.

b) **Who's she?** (Dilma Rousseff)
   _____
   What's she? (a Brazilian politician)
   _____

c) **Who's he?** (Thiago Pereira)
   _____
   What's he? (a Brazilian swimmer)
   _____

d) **Who's he?** (Kaká)
   _____
   What's he? (a famous soccer player)
   _____

Word bank

Who are you?:
Quem é você?
What are you?/
What do you do?
O que você faz?
car racer: piloto de corrida
politician: político
soccer player: jogador de futebol
model: modelo
dentist: dentista
principal: diretor
mailman: carteiro
athlet: atleta
swimmer: nadador

e) **Who's she?** (Gisele Bündchen)

_____

What's she? (a famous Brazilian model)

_____

2 Ask and answer according to the example:

a) **Paul: I am Paul, and you, who are you?**
Mary: I am Mary.
Paul: What are you, Mary?
Mary (a student): I am a student.

b) Robert: _____

Marisa: _____

Robert: _____

Marisa (a singer): _____

3 **A** ou **an**?

a) _____ elephant

b) _____ swimmer

c) _____ airplane

d) _____ boy

e) _____ girls

f) _____ athletes

4 Answer the questions:

a) What's your name?

_____

b) What's your teacher's name?

_____

c) What's the name of your school?

_____

5 Make questions:

a) _____

My name is Mary.

b) _____

My surname is Rodrigues.

c) _____

I am fine, thanks.

d) _____

My telephone number is 5555-0555.

fiveteen **15**

6 Write the words in the correct order to make sentences:

a) well – am – I

   I am well.

b) Jane – name – my – is

   _____

c) you – how – are

   _____

d) like – you – I

   _____

e) nice girl – you – are – a

   _____

f) too – am – student – a – I

   _____

ROLE-PLAY – ORAL DRILL

1 A classe sorteia um(a) aluno(a) que convidará um(a) colega para encenar este diálogo:

Classmate 1: Hello! What's your name?

Classmate 2: My name is...

Classmate 1: What's your surname? (or What's your last name?)

Classmate 2: My surname is...

Classmate 1: What are you? (or What do you do? or What's your occupation?)

Classmate 2: I am a...

Classmate 1: Thank you.

Cada aluno escolhe uma das ocupações abaixo e a revela na hora em que participar da encenação.

> teacher, student, football player, swimmer, politician, musician, model, singer, athlete, actor, actress.

2 Que tal encenar o diálogo inicial da lição? Um aluno faz o papel de Wilson e uma aluna o de Jane. Usem os próprios nomes.

Lesson 3
INTERROGATIVE FORM OF VERB TO BE; ADJECTIVES

Jeff on the bass. **Bob** on the guitar. **Rose** is the vocalist. **Mike** on the trumpet.

An interview

Reporter: Who are you?
Musician: We are musicians.
Reporter: What's the name of your band?
Musician: Everybody knows.
We are very famous!
We are The Crazy Band!
Reporter: The Crazy Band?
Musician: Yes, The Crazy Band!
Reporter: Can you play a song for me?
Musician: Sure. Listen.
Reporter: Oh, you are terrible!
Musicians: We are not terrible. We are modern musicians.

TEXT COMPREHENSION

1 Write true (**T**) or false (**F**) according to the dialogue:

(_____) Jeff plays the bass.

(_____) The name of the band is Crazy Boys.

(_____) Rose is the vocalist of the band.

(_____) The Crazy Band plays a song for the reporter.

2 Answer the questions about the text:

a) What is the name of the band?
_____

b) Are the musicians modern?
_____

c) Who is the singer of The Crazy Band?
_____

d) Who plays the guitar?
_____

e) What is the name of the bass player?
_____

LEARN THIS

1. Observe estas formas verbais:

Singular ⟶ Plural

I am (eu sou, eu estou) ⟶ **We are** (nós somos, nós estamos)

You are (você é, você está) ⟶ **You are** (vocês são, vocês estão)

He is (ele é, ele está)
She is (ela é, ela está) ⟶ **They are** (eles/elas são ou estão)
It is (ele, ela é ou está)

We are (Nós somos, nós estamos)

You are (Você é, você está, vocês são, vocês estão)

Note que o pronome **you** tem uma só forma para dar ideia de singular ou plural. Tanto no singular como no plural, a forma verbal que acompanha o pronome é sempre **are**.

2. Interrogative form of verb to be.

Para fazer perguntas em inglês, colocamos o verbo **to be** antes do sujeito:

You are a teacher. (forma afirmativa)

Are you a teacher? (forma interrogativa)

3. O adjetivo, em inglês, é invariável e vem antes do substantivo:

Singular	Plural
Good boy	Good boys
Good girl	Good girls
Good teacher	Good teachers

4. O artigo **a** (**an**) não é usado no plural.
I am a musician.
We are musicians.

5. Em inglês, o plural dos substantivos se faz geralmente acrescentando-se **s** ao singular:
band – bands
musician – musicians

6. What do you do? Esta expressão significa: O que você faz?/Qual é a sua profissão?

ACTIVITIES

1 Match the pictures with the occupations.

- student
- nurse
- fireman/firefighter
- soccer player
- mechanic
- teacher
- doctor
- painter
- dentist
- singer

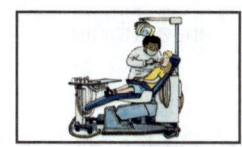

nineteen **19**

2 Write in the plural.

a) I am a musician.
___

b) I am a famous singer.
___

c) You are a crazy boy.
___

d) You are a good student.
___

e) Mary is a nice girl.
Mary and Jane ___

f) She is a nice girl.
___

g) He is a good teacher.
___

h) It is a smart dog.
___

3 Write in the interrogative form.

a) You are musicians.
___

b) Peter is a reporter.
___

c) You can play a song for me.
___

d) You are crazy.
___

e) You are a farmer.
___

f) Fred and Jim are lazy workers.
___

g) The teacher is intelligent.
___

4 Write the dialogue in the correct order.

I am a doctor. _____

What's your name? _____

What's your occupation? _____

My name is David. _____

5 Complete the sentences with the words from the box.

> crazy – are – your – what's – very – play

a) Who _____ you?

b) _____ the name of _____ band?

c) We are _____ famous.

d) Can you _____ a song?

e) You are _____

LISTEN AND WRITE – DICTATION

a) _____ are you? _____ the _____ of _____ ?

b) _____ are _____ .

   _____ in The _____ .

FUN TIME

1 Translate to English.

Crossword
1. maluco
2. músicos
3. famoso, famosa
4. tocar
5. música

A smart goalkeeper

2 Complete the crossword puzzle according to the pictures:

3 Unscramble the words below:

a) ybo _____

b) koob _____

c) rigl _____

d) paml _____

22 twenty-two

4 Word ladder

a) menino
b) lâmpada
c) alô
d) laranja
e) professor
f) avião
g) secretária
h) profissão (ocupação)

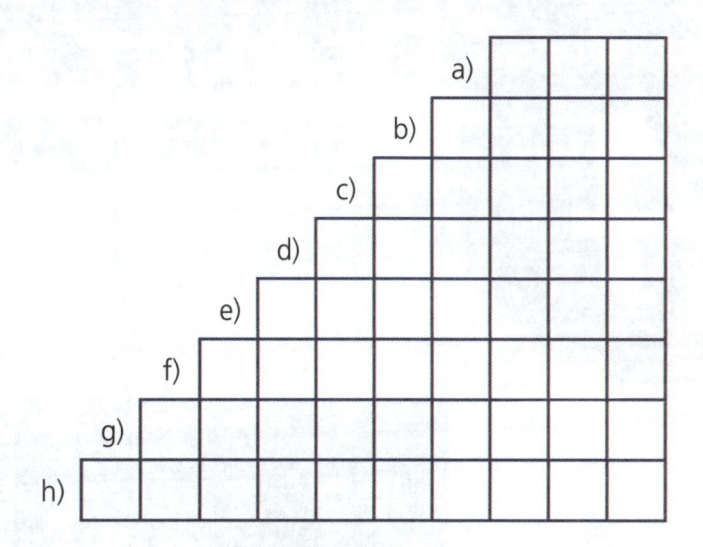

LET'S SING

HAPPY BIRTHDAY

Hap-py birth-day to you, Hap-py birth-day to you! Hap-py birth-day, dear Ma-ry Happy birth-day to you! Hap-py...

ROLE-PLAY – ORAL DRILL

Now you are the reporter.

Que tal encenar o diálogo inicial da lição? Um aluno ou aluna faz o papel do repórter e outro aluno ou aluna representa um músico da banda.

Lesson 4

DEFINITE ARTICLE; VERB CAN; VERB TO BE

Can I see this photo?

Mike: Can I see this photo?

Kate: Sure you can!

Mike: Who are the boys and the girl in this photo?

Kate: They're my friends.

Mike: Who is the girl in the middle?

Kate: She's Helen.

Mike: And the boy on the left? Who is he?

Kate: He's Philip. He's a good soccer player.

Mike: And who is the boy on the right?

Kate: He's Andrew. He's an intelligent boy.

TEXT COMPREHENSION

1 Choose the correct alternative.
   a) Mike can see the photo.   ( ) Yes   ( ) No
   b) The girl's name is Helen.   ( ) Yes   ( ) No
   c) Andrew is a good football player.   ( ) Yes   ( ) No
   d) The boy on the right is Philip.   ( ) Yes   ( ) No

2 Answer the questions.
   a) Who are the boys in the photo?
      They are _____

   b) Who is a good soccer player?
      _____

   c) Who is an intelligent boy?
      _____

   d) Who is on the left in the photo?
      _____

   e) Who is in the middle of the photo?
      _____

LEARN THIS

1. Definite article (artigo definido):
O artigo definido em inglês é **the**.
The significa o, a, os, as.
The boy: o menino   **The girl**: a menina
The boys: os meninos   **The girls**: as meninas

2. Personal pronouns

Singular	Plural
I (eu) ⟶	**we** (nós)
you (tu, você) ⟶	**you** (vós, vocês)
he (ele)	
she (ela) ⟶	**they** (eles, elas)
it (ele, ela)	

Observação: **he**: refere-se a pessoa do sexo masculino.
            she: refere-se a pessoa do sexo feminino.
            it: o pronome **it** (singular) refere-se a coisa ou a animal e geralmente não se traduz.
            Observe:
            It is a picture. (É um quadro.) **It is a dog**. (É um cachorro.)

3. **Verb to be** (verbo ser, estar)
   Present tense (Presente do indicativo)
   I am (eu sou, eu estou)   **We are** (nós somos, nós estamos)
   You are (você é, você está)   **You are** (vocês são, vocês estão)
   He is (ele é, ele está)
   She is (ela é, ela está) ⟶ **They are** (eles/elas são, estão)
   It is (ele/ela é, está)

   Contracted form of verb to be: Pode-se abreviar o verbo **to be** no presente do indicativo, suprimindo-se a vogal inicial do verbo:

I am	You are	He is	They are
I'm	You're	He's	They're

4. **Verbo can** (verbo poder/conseguir), ex.: **I can swim**. (Eu posso/consigo nadar.)
   He can dance. (Ele pode/consegue dançar.)

   Presente tense
   I can (eu posso)   **We can** (nós podemos)
   You can (você pode)   **You can** (vocês podem)
   He can (ele pode)
   She can (ela pode) ⟶ **They can** (eles/elas podem)
   It can (ele/ela pode)

5. Forma interrogativa com os verbos **to be** e **can**
   Na forma interrogativa, os verbos **to be** e **can** antecedem o sujeito:
   They are my friends.
   Are they my friends?
   He is a good football player.
   Is he a good football player?
   I can see this photo.
   Can I see this photo?
   She can sing.
   Can she sing?
   It can swim?
   Can it swim?

ACTIVITIES

1 Write a, an the or x before singular and plural nouns.

a) _____ picture.   _____ pictures.

b) _____ teacher.   _____ teachers.

c) _____ boy.   _____ boys.

d) _____ intelligent boy.   _____ intelligent boys.

2 Complete with personal pronouns.

a) Hi! _____ 'm Mike. _____ 'm a student.

b) Who is the girl on the left? _____ 's my friend.

c) _____ 'm happy. Today is my birthday.

d) Peter and Mary are my classmates. _____ are my friends.

e) The dog is furious. _____ is furious.

f) Antony is a tennis player. _____ is a tennis player.

3 Choose the correct alternative.

a) _____ is my mother. ( ) She ( ) He ( ) You

b) This is Paul. _____ is my brother. ( ) We ( ) He ( ) I

c) _____ am your new friend. ( ) You ( ) I ( ) We

d) _____ are in this school. ( ) I ( ) He ( ) They

e) You and I are classmates. _____ are at school. ( ) He ( ) I ( ) We

4 Change into plural form.

a) I am a student. _____

b) I am a teacher. _____

c) You are a dentist. _____

d) You are a doctor. _____

e) The boy is on the right. _____

f) He is a pilot. _____

g) She is a smart girl. _____

h) Who is he? _____

i) It is a little dog. _____

j) I am at school now. _____

5 Change to the plural form. Follow the pattern.

   a) She is beautiful.   They are beautiful.

   b) She is a beautiful girl. _____

   c) She is a lovely girl. _____

   d) You are a good boy. _____

6 Change to the interrogative form. Follow the pattern.

   a) He is a good boy.   Is he a good boy?

   b) You are my friend. _____

   c) He is a doctor. _____

   d) She is beautiful. _____

7 Rewrite the sentences in the correct order.

   a) are – they – beautiful   They are beautiful.

   b) girl – she – a – pretty – is _____

   c) player – is – he – footbal – a _____

   d) girl – she – ? – is – a – lovely _____

   e) a – are – teacher – ? – you _____

   f) boy – are – a – good – you _____

8 Answer the questions about you:

   a) Are you a dentist?

   _____

   b) Is your mother a teacher?

   _____

   c) Are you in the 5th grade?

   _____

   d) Are you at school now?

   _____

9 Follow the pattern using can:

   a) open the door.   Can I open the door?

   b) shut the window _____

   c) go with you. _____

   d) speak to you. _____

   e) invite my friend. _____

   f) help you. _____

10 Complete the sentences using the words or expressions below:

- ★ a book
- ★ a picture
- ★ water
- ★ the door
- ★ you
- ★ a letter
- ★ a car
- ★ to school
- ★ English

I can
- write _____
- read _____
- go _____
- paint _____
- shut _____
- drink _____
- help _____
- drive _____
- speak _____

11 Change the sentences into interrogative form follow the pattern.

a) **Paul can help you.**   **Can Paul help you?**

b) You can hear me. _____

c) She can walk. _____

d) You can turn on the radio. _____

e) You can turn off the TV. _____

f) I can smoke here. _____

LISTEN AND WRITE – DICTATION

_____
_____
_____
_____
_____
_____
_____
_____

twenty-nine **29**

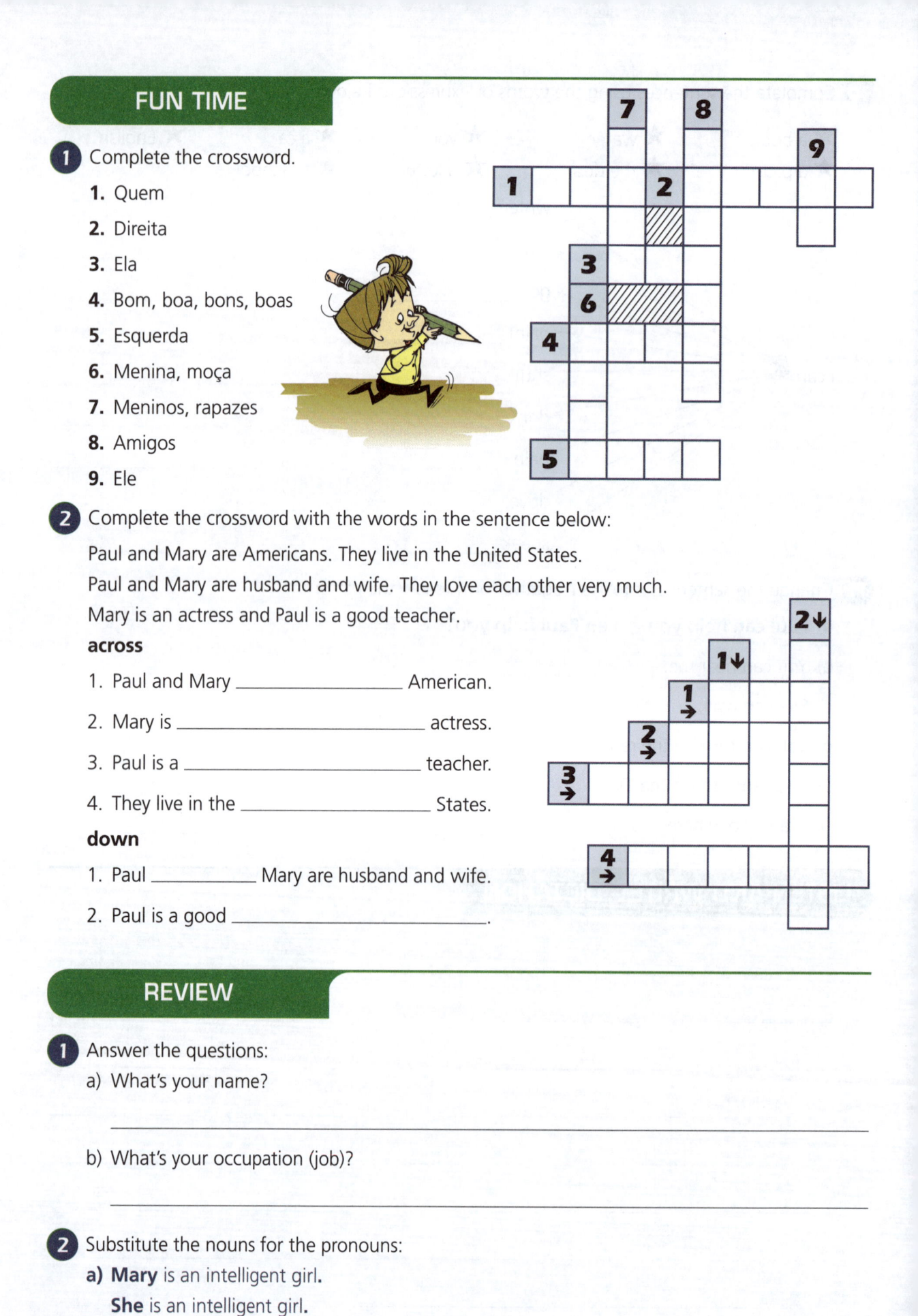

FUN TIME

1 Complete the crossword.

1. Quem
2. Direita
3. Ela
4. Bom, boa, bons, boas
5. Esquerda
6. Menina, moça
7. Meninos, rapazes
8. Amigos
9. Ele

2 Complete the crossword with the words in the sentence below:

Paul and Mary are Americans. They live in the United States.
Paul and Mary are husband and wife. They love each other very much.
Mary is an actress and Paul is a good teacher.

across

1. Paul and Mary _____ American.
2. Mary is _____ actress.
3. Paul is a _____ teacher.
4. They live in the _____ States.

down

1. Paul _____ Mary are husband and wife.
2. Paul is a good _____.

REVIEW

1 Answer the questions:

a) What's your name?
_____

b) What's your occupation (job)?
_____

2 Substitute the nouns for the pronouns:

a) **Mary** is an intelligent girl.
   She is an intelligent girl.

30 thirty

b) **John** likes music.

_____ likes music.

c) **The school** is modern.

_____ is modern.

d) **Apples and oranges** are fruit.

_____ are fruit.

e) **Gina and Peter** are dentists.

_____ are dentists.

f) **Jessica** is on the right in the photo.

_____ is on the right in the photo.

g) **Paul and Mary** are friends.

_____ are friends.

h) **He and she** like vegetables.

_____ like vegetables.

i) **He and I** are in this classroom.

_____ are in this classroom.

3 Complete: the **greetings:**

a) In the morning I say: _____

b) In the afternoon I say: _____

4 Write in the contracted forms of the verb to be:

a) You are good players.   You're good players.

b) She is a nice girl.   _____

c) You are crazy!   _____

d) It is an interesting book.   _____

e) I am an office-boy.   _____

f) He is a doctor.   _____

5 Write in the plural:

a) I am happy.   We are happy.

b) He is a student.   _____

c) Who is she?   _____

Lesson 5
NEGATIVE FORM OF VERB TO BE; OPPOSITE OF ADJECTIVES

Guess who! A guessing game

TV host: Here is a photo of a famous person. Guess who he or she is?
Rose: Is it a man or a woman?
TV host: It's a man.
Jack: Is he young or old?
TV host: He is young.
Ted: Is he rich or poor?
TV host: Oh, he's very rich!
Daisy: Is he a singer or a soccer player?
TV host: He is not a singer. He is a soccer player.
Lucy: Is he a rude or a nice person?
TV host: I think he's nice person.
Paul: Is he Brazilian or English?
TV host: He's Brazilian, of course!
Jim: I think I know his name...
TV host: What's his name? Can you guess who he is?
Jim: He's Rogério Ceni, a famous goalkeeper.
TV host: No, you are wrong! He's not Rogério Ceni.
Kate: I know his name!
TV host: What's his name? Can you guess who he is?
Kate: Sure! He's Kaká. A young and nice soccer player.
TV host: You are right. Take this beautiful poster for you!
Kate: Great!! Thank you!

TEXT COMPREHENSION

1 Answer according to the text:
a) What's the title of the text?

b) Is the famous person poor?

c) Is he English?

d) Is he young?

e) Is the person in the poster rude or nice?

f) Is Jim's answer right?

g) Who guesses the name of the famous person?

h) What's his occupation?

i) Name some qualities of the famous person.

LEARN THIS

1. Interrogative form of the verb to be:
Observe mais uma vez que o verbo **to be** precede o sujeito na forma interrogativa:
He is rich. Is he rich?
They are singers. Are they singers?

2. Negative form

| PRESENT TENSE: TO BE ||
Full form	Contracted form
I am not (Eu não sou/não estou)	I'm not
You are not	You aren't (You're not.)
He is not	He isn't (He's not.)
She is not	She isn't (She's not.)
It is not	It isn't (It's not.)
We are not	We aren't (We're not.)
You are not	You aren't (You're not.)
They are not	They aren't (The're not.)

1. Opposites

Aprenda alguns adjetivos antônimos:

long – short	longo – curto
tall – short	alto – baixo
big – small	grande – pequeno
happy – sad	feliz – triste
kind – rude	gentil – rude
fat – thin	gordo – magro
old – new (coisas)	velho – novo
old – young (pessoas)	velho – novo, jovem
good – bad	bom – mau
dirty – clean	sujo – limpo
beautiful – ugly	bonito – feio
cheap – expensive	atento – descuidado
wrong – right	barato – caro
handsome – ugly	errado – certo
(**handsome** refere-se a homens)	bonito – feio

ACTIVITIES

1 Look at the pictures ask questions and then answer them:

a) the girl

happy or sad

Is this girl happy or sad?

This girl is happy.

She is happy.

b) the car

dirty or clean

_____

_____

_____

c) the boy
lazy or studious

_____

d) the teacher
clever or ignorant

_____

e) the girl
thin or fat?

_____

f) the car
old or new?

_____

2 Answer the questions in the negative form. Use opposites.

a) **Is the girl short?**
   No, she is not short.
   She is tall.

b) Is the teacher fat?

_____

c) Is the car old?

_____

d) Are your hands clean?

_____

e) Are the balls big?

_____

f) Is the street long?

_____

g) Is the house beautiful?

_____

h) Is the man old?

_____

thirty-five **35**

3 Change the sentences to the interrogative and negative forms:

a) Mary is my friend.
   Is Mary my friend?
   No, she is not my friend.

b) We are in the same classroom.
   _____
   _____

c) The teacher is thin.
   _____
   _____

d) The house is big.
   _____
   _____

e) She can speak English.
   _____
   _____

f) You are well.
   _____
   _____

4 Write the opposite.

a) I am old.   I am young.
b) The dog is ugly.   _____
c) The classroom is clean. _____
d) My pencil is short. _____
e) You are wrong.   _____
f) The teacher is tall. _____
g) We are old.   _____

FUN TIME

1 Complete the crossword using the opposites of the underlined adjectives.

a) My friend is very short.
b) Your car is very dirty.
c) Is your teacher old?
d) I am rude.
e) Are you mindless?
f) She is ugly.
g) Your friend is fat.
h) He is very young.

2 Color the doted areas.

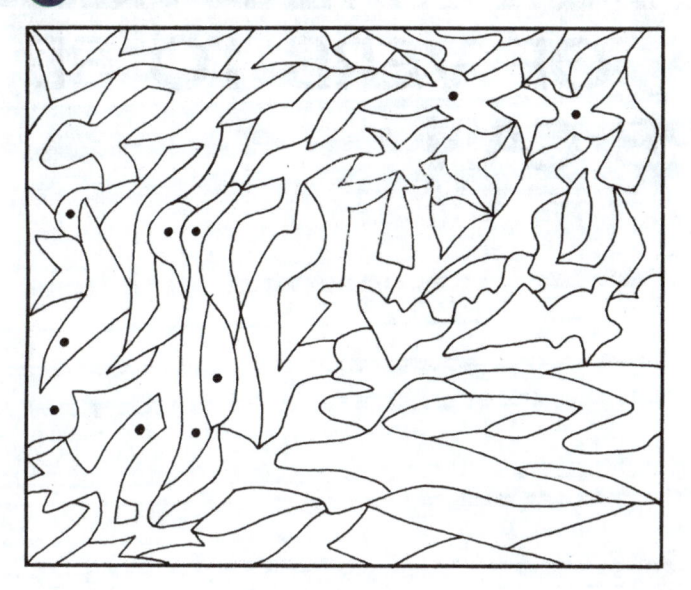

What's hidden in the picture?
Are they things?   ( ) yes   ( ) no
Are they animals? ( ) yes   ( ) no
Are they people?   ( ) yes   ( ) no
What are they?
They are _____.

3 Follow the dots:

> **Word bank**
> **dotted:** pontilhada
> **hidden:** oculto, escondido
> **things:** coisas
> **people:** pessoas
> **follow:** siga
> **dots:** pontos
> **dot to dot:** ponto a ponto

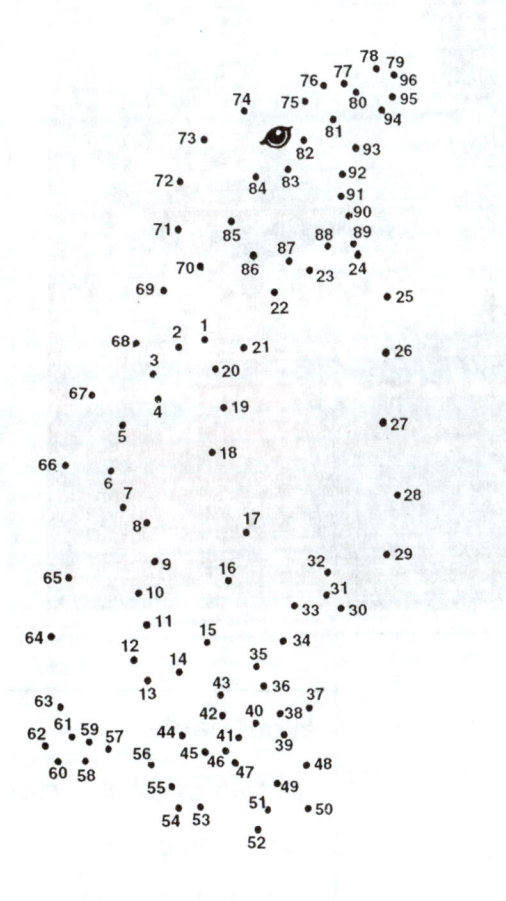

ROLE-PLAY – ORAL DRILL

Que tal fazer um jogral com o diálogo inicial da lição? Organize o seu grupo para representar estes personagens: Entertainer, Rose, Jack, Ted, Daisy, Lucy, Paul, Jim, Kate.

thirty-seven 37

Lesson 6
NEGATIVE FORM OF VERB TO BE AND VERB CAN

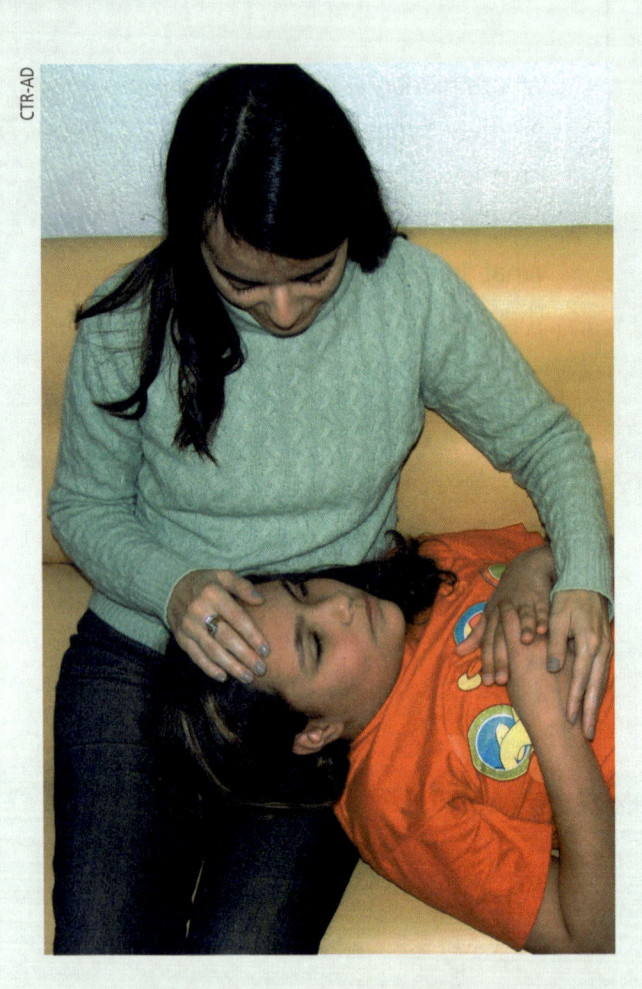

I'm not well, mom…

Mom: Hi, daughter.
Daughter: Hi, mom.
Mom: You seem to be ill…
Daughter: I'm not well, mom…
I've got a terrible headache.
Mom: Poor child.
Let's go to the doctor's.
Daughter: It's not necessary.
Give me some medicine and the headache
will disappear.

Word bank

doctor's office = doctor's: consultório médico

medicine: remédio

mom: mother (tratamento carinhoso para mãe).

I've got = I have got: eu tenho
(Nessa expressão o termo **got** não se traduz).

TEXT COMPREHENSION

1 Choose the correct alternative.

a) The daughter seems to be

( ) well   ( ) ill

b) The headache is

( ) terrible   ( ) bad

c) Who has got a terrible headache?

( ) the mother ( ) the daughter

d) The daughter and the mother go to the doctor's.

( ) yes   ( ) no

e) The headache can disappear with a medicine.

( ) yes   ( ) no

2 Write in English:

– Filha, você parece estar doente...

– Mãe, eu não estou bem. Eu estou doente.

_____

_____

LEARN THIS

1. Verb to be (negative form)

A forma negativa dos verbos **to be** se faz mediante o emprego da palavra **not** após as formas verbais: **am**, **is**, **are**.

Ex.: **I am well.** (Eu estou bem.) **I am not well.** (Eu não estou bem.)

2. Verb can (negative form): o verbo **can** possui só duas formas negativas **cannot** e **can't**.

Ex.: **I cannot guess/I can't guess**. (Eu não posso adivinhar.)

VERB CAN PRESENT TENSE		
Full negative form	**Contracted negative form**	**Interrogative form**
I cannot	I can't	Can I?
You cannot	You can't	Can you?
He cannot	He can't	Can he?
She cannot	She can't	Can she?
It cannot	It can't	Can it?
We cannot	We can't	Can we?
You cannot	You can't	Can you?
They cannot	They can't	Can they?

ACTIVITIES

1 Change the sentences to the negative form. Use full forms of the verb to be:

a) **Mary is my friend.**
   Mary is not my friend.

b) It is necessary.
   _____

c) I can take some medicine.
   _____

d) They are happy.
   _____

e) The room is dirty.
   _____

f) The teacher is young.
   _____

2 Write in the negative contracted form:

a) John is a rude boy. _____

b) Margaret is a thin girl. _____

c) You are careful. _____

d) The cars are expensive. _____

e) We are friends. _____

f) Monica and Linda are mindless. _____

g) I can go to the doctor's. _____

3 Follow the pattern:

a) **Mary – ugly – beautiful.**
   Is Mary ugly?
   No, she is not ugly. She is beautiful.

b) Helen – young – old
   _____
   _____

c) car – old – new
   _____
   _____

d) boys – kind – rude
   _____
   _____

e) books – cheap – expensive
   _____
   _____

4 Write in English:

a) Eu não estou bem. Eu estou doente.
   _____

b) Não é necessário.
   _____

LISTEN AND WRITE – DICTATION

_____
_____
_____
_____
_____

FUN TIME

1 Complete the crossword in English.
  a) **The book is** (barato).
  b) **Mary is** (atenta).
  c) **Gordon is** (alto).
  d) **Richard is** (gentil).
  e) **The car is** (novo).
  f) **It is** (limpo).
  g) **He is very** (rude).
  h) **It is a** (grande) **school**.

REVIEW

1 Complete the dialogue.

Good afternoon.
_____

How are you?
_____

What's your name?
_____

What's your occupation?
_____

Are you English?
_____

Nice to meet you!
_____

Match the opposites of these adjectives:

- rude •
- young •
- ugly •
- dirty •
- cheap •
- good •
- tall •

- • expensive
- • short
- • kind
- • old
- • beautiful
- • clean
- • bad

forty-one **41**

3 Write the plural.

a) I am a good student.
_____

b) She is a beautiful girl.
_____

c) It is an expensive book.
_____

d) He is an old doctor.
_____

4 Change the sentences to the interrogative form.

a) She is kind.
_____

b) You can help me.
_____

c) You are well.
_____

d) She can sing this song.
_____

e) The car is clean.
_____

f) They can speak English.
_____

5 Change the sentences to the negative form.

a) You are my friend.
_____

b) We can study at night.
_____

c) I can speak English.
_____

d) It is expensive.
_____

e) We are ill.
_____

6 Write dirty or clean according to the pictures:

a) _____ b) _____ c) _____ d) _____

7 Write young or old according to the pictures:

a) _____ b) _____ c) _____ d) _____

42 forty-two

8 Write tall, high and short according to the pictures.

a) _____ boy.   b) _____ boy.   c) _____ mountain.   d) _____ hair.

ROLE-PLAY – ORAL DRILL

Junte-se a um/a colega e treinem um dos diálogos a seguir. Depois apresente-o à classe.

Os diálogos são baseados no texto inicial desta lição: uma aluna faz o papel da mãe **(mom)** e uma aluna ou um aluno o papel de uma filha **(daughter)** ou de um filho **(son)** doente. As doenças variam em cada diálogo: **headache** (dor de cabeça), **stomachache** (dor de estômago), **backache** (dor nas costas), **earache** (dor de ouvido). Façam gestos e expressões de quem está com dor de cabeça, ou de estômago, ou dor nas costas, ou dor de ouvido. Façam uma encenação divertida.

Diálogo A – Headache

Mom: Hi, daughter!

Son/Daughter: Hi, mom.

Mom: You seem to be ill...

Son/Daughter: I'm not well, mom.

Mom: What's the problem?

Son/Daughter: I've got a terrible headache!

Mom: Oh! Poor child! Let's go to the doctor's.

Dialogue B – Stomachache

Você vai mudar as palavras para **terrible stomachache** e fazer os gestos e expressões de uma terrível dor de estômago.

Dialogue C – Backache

Você vai mudar as palavras para **terrible backache** e fazer os gestos e expressões de uma terrível dor nas costas.

Dialogue D – Earache

Você vai mudar as palavras para **terrible earache** e fazer os gestos e expressões de uma terrível dor de ouvido.

Lesson 7
Demonstrative pronouns: this, that

A strange plumber

1. Help! It's an emergency!

2. Fred, is that the house? — Yes, it is. Look at the water!

3. We're in trouble. Look at the ocean! The problem is in this tube.

4. I'm hungry. Excuse me! It's my lunch time! — Help!

5. He's a very strange plumber!

TEXT COMPREHENSION

1 What is the title of the cartoon?
_____

2 Is this text comic or serious?
_____

3 A plumber repairs...
( ) cars ( ) television sets ( ) water pipes, bathtubs, sinks...

4 The problem happens...
( ) in a house ( ) in an apartment

5 Who is nervous with the situation?
( ) a baby ( ) a girl ( ) a man and a woman

6 The strange plumber is...
( ) a nervous person ( ) a calm person

7 Is the strange plumber thin or fat?
_____

8 Who helps the strange plumber?
_____

9 Who is hungry?
_____

10 Who stops the work to eat?
_____

11 The strange plumber stops the work to eat because...
( ) it is his lunch time ( ) it is his dinner time

Word bank

repair: consertar
water pipe: cano de água
bathroom: banheiro
sink: pia
help: ajudar
stop: parar
work: trabalho; trabalhar
eat: comer
because: porque
lunch: almoço
dinner: jantar

LEARN THIS

1. Demonstrative pronouns
This – That

This is my kite.
That is my kite.

This é usado para pessoa, animal ou objeto que esteja perto.
This significa: este, esta, isto.
That é usado para algo ou alguém, afastado de quem fala.
That significa: aquele, aquela, aquilo.

forty-five

ACTIVITIES

1 Observe the pictures and answer the questions.

Is this a book or a magazine?
_____

Is that the Moon or a star?
_____

Is this a stick or a tube?
_____

Is that a ship or a boat in the ocean?
_____

Is this a bus or a train?
_____

Is that a kite or a bird?
_____

2 Answer the questions according to the pictures.

a) **Is this mother happy or unhappy?**
This mother is happy.
She is happy.

b) Is this boy scared or angry?
_____
_____

c) Is this boy happy or unhappy?
_____
_____

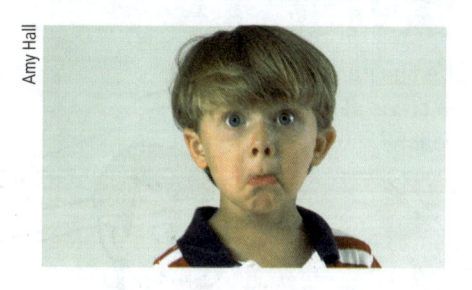

d) Is this isle big or small?
_____
_____

LET'S SING

My little house

I have a little house.
My house is white and blue.
It has a large door
For my friends, for you.

My house is poor indeed
But people are rich in it:
They have food, love and peace.

My house has a garden, too.
It`s for my friends, it`s for you.

Antes de cantar a música, ouça o professor ou o CD. Preste atenção na pronúncia das palavras.

Lesson 8

Demonstrative adjectives: these, those

Visiting Rio de Janeiro

What's the name of those trees along the beach?

These trees are called chapéu-de-sol. Chapéu is hat and Sol is sun. They are named this way because they protect people from the sun.

Thank you. And what is that big statue on the top of that mount?

That's Cristo Redentor, a famous statue in Rio de Janeiro. It's called Christ, the Redeemer. It's one of the Wonders of the world!

Oh! That's wonderful! Let's go there! Let's go there!

TEXT COMPREHENSION

1. Where are the tourists? _____

2. Where are the trees called "chapéu-de-sol"? _____

3. The trees "chapéu-de-sol" protect people from?
   ( ) the fire   ( ) the sun   ( ) the wind

4. Complete:
   The Cristo Redentor is a _____ on the top _____ in Rio de Janeiro.

forty-nine 49

LEARN THIS

Demonstratives

Singular	Plural	Singular	Plural
This	These	That	Those
este	estes	aquele	aqueles
esta	estas	aquela	aquelas
isto		aquilo	

What are these?   These are pictures.   What are those?   Those are birds.

Observações

Note:

What are these? (O que são estas coisas?)

These are pictures. (Estas coisas são figuras).

What are those? (O que são aqueles?)

Those are birds. (Aqueles são pássaros).

Observe:

This is a pen.

These are pens.

That is an orange.

Those are oranges.

O artigo **a** ou **an** desaparece no plural.

Plural dos substantivos: o plural, em inglês, forma-se geralmente acrescentando-se **s** ao singular. Exemplos: **boy**, **boys**, **car**, **cars**, **book**, **books**.

ACTIVITIES

1 Write the sentences in the singular and in the plural forms.

Cat

This is a Cat.

_____

_____

Diver

This is _____

_____

_____

Tourist

_____

_____

_____

2 Look at the example and continue the exercise.

a) **Mount – high**
   That mount is high.
   That is a high mount.
   →
   Mounts – high
   Those mounts are high.
   Those are high mounts.

b) tourist – English → tourists – English

_____ _____

_____ _____

c) house – big → houses – big

_____ _____

_____ _____

d) statue – famous → statues – famous

_____ _____

_____ _____

fifty-one **51**

3 Answer the questions according to the pictures.

a) **Are these magazines?**
   No, they are not.
   They are books.

b) Are those oranges?
   _____
   _____

c) Are those apples?
   _____
   _____

d) Are these cats?
   _____
   _____

e) Are these pencils?
   _____
   _____

f) Are those balloons?
   _____
   _____

4 Color the picture and write sentences using the words that and those:

_____
_____
_____
_____

LISTEN AND WRITE – DICTATION

_____ the name _____ along _____ beach?
_____ big statue _____ mount?

52 fifty-two

FUN TIME

5 Rewrite these interrogative sentences in the correct order:

a) those things – what – Mom – in the sky – are

b) in the sky – What – that – is

_____ Those things are stars.

_____ That is a balloon.

6 A plural crossword puzzle:
Complete the crossword according to the pictures:

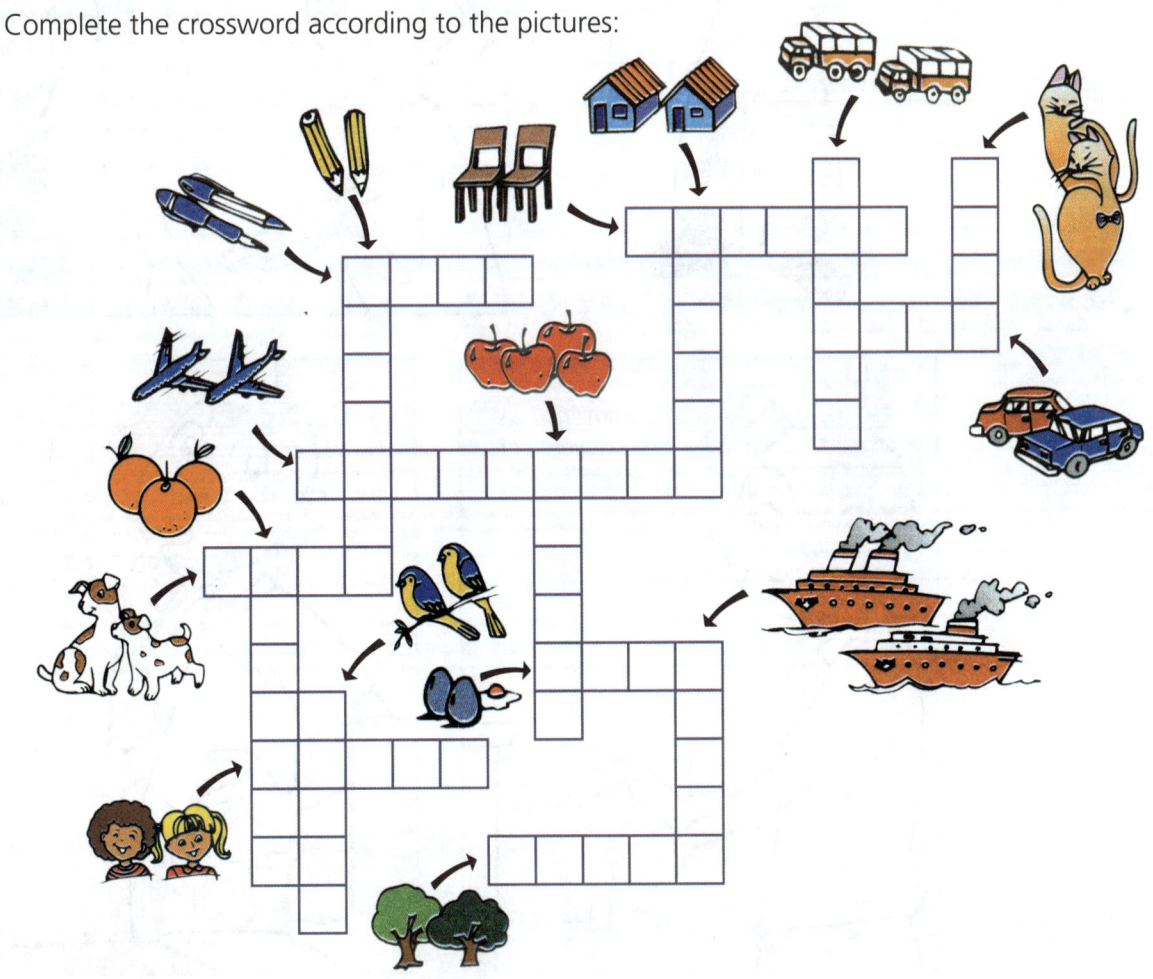

Lesson 9
PREPOSITIONS IN, ON, UNDER; INTERROGATIVE WORD WHERE

Where's my cell phone?

- Where's my cell phone?
- Where's my cell phone, mom?
- Your cell phone? Is it on the table? Look in the drawer.
- It's not in the drawer.
- Is it in the bedroom?
- On the bed...
- Where?

fifty-five 55

TEXT COMPREHENSION

1 Answer according to the text.

a) Who is looking for a cell phone? _____

b) Is the cell phone under the bed? _____

c) Who finally finds the cell phone? _____

d) Where is it? _____

2 Write true (**T**) or false (**F**) according to the text.

( ) The cell phone is not in the drawer.

( ) The cell phone is in the drawer.

( ) The cell phone is not on the table.

( ) The cell phone is on the table.

( ) The cell phone is in the cupboard.

( ) The cell phone is under the pillow.

( ) The cell phone is on the pillow.

3 Name the places where Jack and his mother look for the cell phone.

LEARN THIS

1. Prepositions in, on, under

Observe o emprego dessas preposições em inglês:

in (em, dentro de)

The cell phone is in the pocket. (O celular está dentro do bolso).

The boy is in the car. (O menino está no carro).

on (sobre, em cima de)

That cell phone is on the chair. (O celular está sobre a cadeira).

The English book is on the table. (O livro de inglês está sobre a mesa).

under (sob, embaixo de)

The dog is under the table. (O cachorro está embaixo da mesa).

The cat is under the bed. (O gato está embaixo da cama).

2. Observe o emprego da palavra interrogativa **where**:

Where is the cell phone? (Onde está o telefone celular?)

Where are the cats? (Onde estão os gatos?)

A hungry cat

Where is the little mouse?
Where is the little mouse?
I am so hungry!
I want to eat it
With my big mouth!

Is it in the box?
No, it is not.
Is it in the shoe?
No, it is not.

Where is the little mouse?
Where is the little mouse?
I am so hungry!
I want to eat it
With my big mouth!
Is it under the table?

No, it is not.
Is it under the bed?
No, it is not.

Where is the little mouse?
Where is the little mouse?
I am so hungry!
I want to eat it
With my big mouth!

Is it on the chair?
No, it is not.
Is it on the stove?
No, it is not.
Where is the little mouse?

I am hungry. Where is the little mouse?

TEXT COMPREHENSION

1) Write (F) for false or (T) for true according to the text:

a) The mouse is big. ( ) ( )

b) The cat`s mouth is big. ( ) ( )

c) The mouse is in the shoe. ( ) ( )

d) The mouse is under the table. ( ) ( )

e) The cat is hungry. ( ) ( )

f) The text says where the little mouse is. ( ) ( )

ACTIVITIES

1 Write in English.

a) Onde está o gato? _____

b) O rato está sobre a caixa. _____

c) O gato está embaixo da mesa. _____

2 Look at the example and answer the questions.

a) **Where is your mother? (at home)**
She is at home. (My mother is at home.)

b) Where is your teacher? (at school)

_____

c) Where is the president? (in Brasília)

_____

d) Where are you? (here)

_____

3 Look at the picture and answer the questions.

a) Where is the dog?

_____

b) Where are the cows?

_____

c) Where are the pencils?

_____

d) Where is the book?

_____

58 fifty-eight

4 Who is hungry: the mouse or the cat? _____

5 Translate:

The cat is hungry. It is not angry. _____

6 Indicate the places where the cat looks for the mouse. _____

7 Draw the pictures of a little mouse and a big mouth.

8 Write the words in the correct order and make sentences:

a) the – ? – is – under – bed – it _____

b) big – with – eat – mouse – the – my – mouth – ! – I _____

c) so – am – I – ! – hungry _____

d) the – it – stove – ? – is – on _____

9 Find these words in English in the word-hunt:

travesseiro – cama – mesa – quarto – onde – fogão

W	R	W	A	T	C	H	U	O	N	P	G	S	C	N	N	P	L
T	I	B	D	X	X	B	E	D	R	O	O	M	B	B	E	D	X
A	P	B	E	C	K	L	M	B	U	U	I	F	C	D	D	P	L
P	P	I	L	L	O	W	V	O	C	I	D	D	P	L	M	N	H
W	Y	X	Z	I	C	S	T	O	V	E	Y	D	V	M	V	H	P
S	X	J	K	R	V	M	N	W	H	E	R	E	T	E	B	S	W
G	B	B	T	W	T	A	B	L	E	Y	U	I	M	T	G	D	C

Palm tree, sun, hat, shrub, tail of the tiger.

10 Search the differences between these pictures. How many?

Lesson 10
CARDINAL NUMBERS; CLOTHES; COLORS

13

In a shop

Mrs. Stores enters in a shop to buy clothes.

Let me see that black shirt. How much is it?

It costs ten dollars.

Ten dollars? It's expensive!

Oh, no! It's cheap!

Let me see that yellow blouse. How much is it?

It costs nine dollars.

Nine dollars? It's expensive!

Oh, no! It's cheap!

Let me see that blue skirt. How much is it?

It costs eight dollars.

Eight dollars? It's expensive!

Oh, no! It's cheap!

Let me see that red dress. How much is it?
It costs seven dollars.
Seven dollars? It's expensive!
Oh, no! It's cheap!
And those slacks?
Ten dollars!
Oh, they are expensive!
These socks are cheap, they cost one dollar...
One dollar? They are expensive!
BARGAIN SHOP
It's expensive!

TEXT COMPREHENSION

1 According to the text, who enters the shop?
_____

2 Mrs. Stores enters a shop.
( ) to buy a pair of shoes.
( ) to buy a purse.
( ) to buy clothes.

> **Word bank**
> **slacks**: calças (geralmente esportivas)
> **pants** (EUA)/**trousers** (Inglaterra): calças (geralmente de homem)

3 The shopkeeper is:
( ) a man.   ( ) a woman.

4 According to the shopkeeper, the clothes:
( ) are cheap.   ( ) are expensive.

5 According to Mrs. Stores, the clothes:
( ) are cheap.   ( ) are expensive.

6 How much are the clothes below?
a) The black shirt costs _____
b) The yellow blouse costs _____
c) The blue skirt costs _____
d) The red dress costs _____
e) The slacks cost _____
f) The socks cost _____

Observações

enters – costs

A maioria dos verbos em inglês recebe um s na terceira pessoa do singular do presente do indicativo:

Ela entra... – **She enters**...

Este custa... – **This costs**...

7 Complete with enters, enter, costs or cost:
a) We _____ in a shop (enters – enter).
b) She _____ in a shop (enters – enter).
c) These socks _____ ten dollars (costs – cost).
d) That blouse _____ twenty dollars (costs – cost).
e) This t-shit _____ nine dollars (costs – cost).

62   sixty-two

NUMBERS

1 Writing the numbers.

Numbers from 1 to 20

1: one	11: eleven
2: two	12: twelve
3: three	13: thirteen
4: four	14: fourteen
5: five	15: fifteen
6: six	16: sixteen
7: seven	17: seventeen
8: eight	18: eighteen
9: nine	19: nineteen
10: ten	20: twenty

20 = twenty
21 twenty-one
22 twenty-two
23 twenty-three
24 _____

30 = thirty
31 _____
32 _____
33 _____
34 _____

40 = forty
41 _____
42 _____
43 _____
44 _____
45 _____

50 = fifty
51 _____
57 _____
58 _____

60 = sixty
61 _____
66 _____

70 = seventy
71 _____
72 _____
73 _____

80 = eighty
81 _____
82 _____
83 _____

90 = ninety
91 _____
92 _____

100 = a hundred / one hundred
105 _____
200 _____
500 _____
900 _____

1000 = one thousand

sixty-three **63**

ADDITION
+ and/plus

2 Add the numbers:

a) 1 + 2 = 3   one and two is three

b) 5 + 2 = ☐ _____

c) 10 + 19 = ☐ _____

d) 40 + 15 = ☐ _____

SUBTRACTION
− minus

3 Subtract the numbers:

a) 5 − 3 = 2   five minus three is two

b) 30 − 12 = ☐ _____

c) 80 − 4 = ☐ _____

d) 19 − 3 = ☐ _____

MULTIPLICATION
× multiplied by/times

4 Multiply the numbers:

a) 2 × 3 = 6   two times three is six

b) 6 × 4 = ☐ _____

c) 7 × 8 = ☐ _____

d) 8 × 9 = ☐ _____

DIVISION
÷ divided by

5 Divide the numbers:

a) 10 ÷ 2 = 5   ten divided by two is five

b) 36 ÷ 3 = ☐ _____

c) 15 ÷ 3 = ☐ _____

d) 35 ÷ 7 = ☐ _____

6 Look at the prices and answer the questions.

a) U$ 5.20

How much is this t-shirt?
It's five dollars and twenty cents.

d) U$ 25.00

How much are these glasses?
They are twenty-five dollars.

b) U$ 10.35

How much is this CD?
_____

e) U$ 30.00

How much are these shoes?
_____

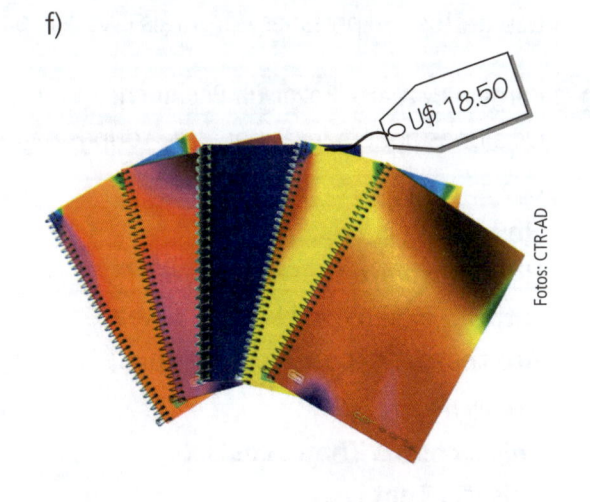

c) U$ 15.00

How much is this calculator?
_____

f) U$ 18.50

How much are these copybooks?
_____

7 Match the columns:

- socks
- shoes
- a dress
- a jacket
- a green shirt
- a yellow skirt
- trousers
- blue tennis shoes
- blue shorts
- a brown blouse

ROLE-PLAY – ORAL DRILL

1 Vamos encenar o texto *In a shop*?
Organize um grupo com três personagens:
– Um aluno faz o papel de narrador.
– Uma aluna faz o papel de Mrs. Stores.
– Um aluno faz o papel do vendedor (**shopkeeper**).
Use gestos e expressões corporais e vocais para enriquecer sua encenação.

2 Bargain Bazaar – Bazar da Pechincha.
Os alunos podem levar peças de roupas para a classe e encenar um comércio de roupas.

Use as perguntas:
How much is this.../that...?
How much are these.../those...?
Is this... expensive? Is this... cheap?
Are these... expensive? Are those... cheap?

Use as respostas:
This... costs... That... costs...
This is... That is...
These cost... Those cost...
These are... Those are...

LISTEN AND WRITE – DICTATION

FUN TIME

1 Crossing numbers

	70	100		80			60	
			50					90
						10		
			30					
20								
				40				

2 Adding fun
Use numbers from zero to seven in each empty square so that their total is twelve. You can't repeat the same number.

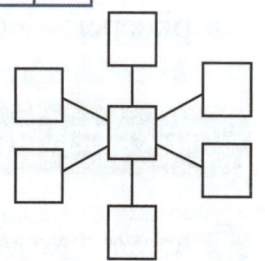

LET'S SING

Little Indians
One little, two little, three little Indians,
Four little, five little, six little Indians,
Seven little, eight little, nine little Indians,
Ten little Indian boys.

sixty-seven **67**

REVIEW

In a bookshop

Shopkeeper: Can I help you?
Customer: Oh, yes. How much is this book?
Shopkeeper: It costs ten dollars.
Customer: And this magazine about sports? How much is it?
Shopkeeper: It costs seven dollars and twenty-five cents.
Customer: Ok.
Shopkeeper: Anything else?
Customer: No, thank you. How much are the book and the magazine?
Shopkeeper: They are seventeen dollars and twenty-five cents.
Customer: Here you are. Twenty dollars.
Shopkeeper: Here is your change: two dollars and seventy-five cents.
Customer: Ok. Thank you.
Shopkeeper: You're welcome.

Word bank
shopkeeper: lojista
customer: freguês
costs: custa
magazine: revista
Here you are: aqui está
change: troco
You're welcome: de nada

TEXT COMPREHENSION

1 Answer the questions:

a) What is the magazine about? _____

b) How much is the book? _____

c) How much is the change? _____

2 Write "Yes, it is or "No, it isn't":

a) The book is about sports. _____

b) The magazine is 7.25 dollars. _____

c) The book is 17.25 dollars. _____

d) The change is 2.55 dollars. _____

Lesson 11
Affirmative and interrogative forms of verb there to be

On a farm

Look at the picture listen the CD and answer the questions orally:

a) How many boats can you see on the lake?

b) How many ducks are there on the lake?

c) How many houses are there on the farm?

d) How many cows or bulls can you see in the picture?

e) How many trucks are there in the picture?

f) How many boys are there in the picture?

g) How many cowboys are there in the picture?

LEARN THIS

Verb there to be (verbo haver)
There is: há (singular)
There are: há (plural)
Is there?: há? (singular)
Are there?: há? (plural)
A expressão **how many** significa quantos(as) e se refere a seres contáveis*.

ACTIVITIES

1 Answer the questions:

a) How many people are there in your family? _____
b) How many doors are there in your house? _____
c) How many windows are there in your classroom? _____
d) How many books are there in your schoolbag? _____
e) How many fingers are there in your hand? _____

2 Follow the pattern:

a) bees – on the flower

How many bees are there on the flower?

b) beds – in the bedroom
_____

c) desks – in the classroom
_____

d) copybooks – in the bag
_____

3 Look at the picture, make a question and give an answer:

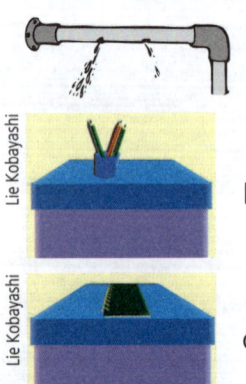

holes – in the pipe

pens – on the desk

copybooks – on the desk

a) **How many holes are there in the pipe?**
   There are two holes in the pipe.

b) _____
   _____

c) _____
   _____

4 Complete with there is, there are, is there or are there.

a) _____ a cat under the bed?
b) _____ four pens on the table.
c) _____ two birds in the nest?
d) _____ ten students in the classroom.
e) _____ a girl in the car?
f) _____ a mouse in the box.

FUN TIME

a) Write the year of your birth. _____

b) Double it. _____

c) Multiply by 50. _____

d) Add your age. _____

If you have solved this problem correctly, the year of your birth is on the left and your age is on the right.

ROLE-PLAY – ORAL DRILL

You are the actor. Leia o texto para os colegas em voz alta, usando gestos, entonação e voz de suspense.

A Thrilling Poem

In the green forest
there is an old house.
In the old house
there is a dark room.
In the dark room
there is a wardrobe.
In the wardrobe
there is a black box.
In the black box
there is a ......
ghost!

Answer according to the text:

a) What color is the forest?
_____

b) What color is the room?
_____

c) What color is the box?
_____

d) Where is the old house?
_____

e) Where is the dark room?
_____

f) Where is the wardrobe?
_____

g) Where is the ghost?
_____

h) What is the meaning of the word thrilling?
_____

Lesson 12

AFFIRMATIVE AND NEGATIVE FORMS OF VERB CAN

A bird and a nest

Chris and Mike are on vacation on a farm.

Chris: Mike, what is that in the tree?
Mike: It's a nest.
Chris: Let's see what's in it?
Mike: Yes!
Chris: Can you climb the tree?
Mike: Sure. I can!
   (And Mike climbs the tree.)
Mike: Oh! There are four little eggs in the nest!
Chris: Look! The mother bird is near the nest! Don't touch the eggs! Respect nature!
Mike: Ok. I can't touch the eggs because the mother bird might abandon the nest.

TEXT COMPREHENSION

1 Write true (T) or false (F) according to the text:

a) Betty and Mike are on vacation. ( )
b) There is a bird in the nest. ( )
c) Mike can climb the tree. ( )
d) There are five eggs in the nest. ( )
e) If Mike touches the eggs the mother bird might abandon the nest. ( )

2 Answer the questions:

a) Where are Chris and Mike?
___

b) Where is the nest?
___

c) Who climbs the tree?
___

d) How many eggs are there in the nest?
___

e) Is the mother bird near or far from the nest?
___

f) Chris gives a good advice to Mike. What is it?
___

LEARN THIS

Verb can

1. O verbo **can** é auxiliar. Significa poder, no sentido de capacidade física ou mental. Não recebe **s** na 3ª pessoa do singular do presente do indicativo.

2. Present tense

I can (eu posso...)
You can (você pode...)
He can (ele pode...)
She can (ela pode...)
It can (ele pode...)

We can (nós podemos...)
You can (vocês podem...)
They can (eles podem...)

3. Can possui duas formas negativas: **cannot** e **can't**

ACTIVITIES

1 Write the sentences under the corresponding pictures.
- The baby can walk now.
- I can swim.
- Bob can't walk now.
- Jane can't swim.

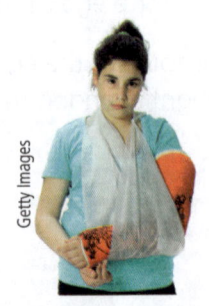

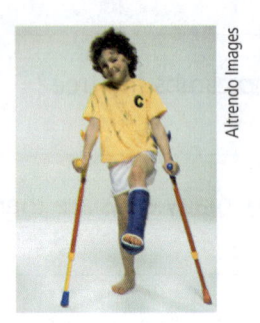

_____   _____

_____   _____

2 Answer the questions. Choose the answers here.

I can write.   I can touch.
I can speak.   I can hear.
I can eat.   I can work.
I can see.   I can smell.

a) What can you do with your hands?
I can touch.
_____
_____

b) What can you do with your nose?
_____
_____

c) What can you do with your mouth?
_____
_____

d) What can you do with your eyes?
_____

e) What can you do with your ears?
_____

74 seventy-four

3 Let's have fun! Can you guess what I am?

Toad   Table    Lion

I have four legs and a tail.
I can roar.
You can see me in the zoo.
What am I?

You are a _____

Dog   Chair     Boy

I have four legs.
I cannot walk.
You can sit on me.
What am I?

You are a _____

Kite   Cat    Duck

I have a long string.
I have a tail.
You can make me fly in the wind.
What am I?

You are a _____

Piano   Door    Zebra

I have many keys.
They are black and white.
You can play music on me.
What am I?

You are a _____

ROLE-PLAY – ORAL DRILL

Junte sete colegas e organize um jogral com o texto. Há oito versos nas duas estrofes. Cada um recita um verso. Procure pronunciar bem as palavras e dar entonação na voz.

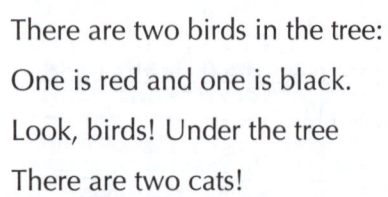

There are two birds in the tree:
One is red and one is black.
Look, birds! Under the tree
There are two cats!

There is a nest in the tree.
There is an egg in the nest.
There is a bird in the egg.
Don't touch it yet.

TEXT COMPREHENSION

Answer according to the text:

a) What is dangerous for the two birds? _____

b) How many birds can you see in the tree? _____

c) How many eggs are there in the nest? _____

d) What color are the birds? _____

e) What color is the egg? _____

REVIEW

1 Write in the negative form.

Negative form of **can** → can't / can not / cannot

a) **She can walk.**
   She can't walk

b) I can see.
   _____

c) I can read.
   _____

d) The old man can run.
   _____

e) The bird can swim.
   _____

2 Change to the interrogative form.

a) **You can see a bird.**
   Can you see a bird?

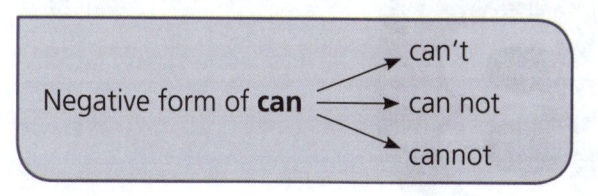

b) She can write.
   _____

c) The baby can walk.
   _____

d) You can speak English.
   _____

e) He can eat an apple.
   _____

f) She can read this letter.
   _____

3 Complete the balloons with these expressions: play soccer, cross the street, swim, read a book, drive a car, write your name.

Can you play soccer?
Yes, we can.

_____ they _____ ?
Yes, _____

_____ she _____ ?
Yes, _____

_____ you _____ ?
Yes, _____

_____ you _____ ?
Yes, _____

_____ you _____ ?
Yes, _____

Lesson 13
How old are you?

How old are you?

A
- How old are you? Are you eighteen?
- Yes, I am. I am eighteen years old.
- And I am nineteen.
- MOVIE
- Under 18 are not admitted

B
- Congratulations! How old are you, sir?
- How are you so strong?
- Old?... I am young! I am only seventy years old!
- Natural food!

C
- How old are you, sir?
- How old are you? How old are you?
- Pardon??? I am not Harold. I am Arnold.
- Ah... How old am I? I am only eighty. But my mother is ninety-nine!

TEXT COMPREHENSION

Answer according to the texts.

Text A
a) How old the boy? _____
b) And the girl? How old is she? _____

Text B
a) How old is the runner? _____
b) Is the runner young or old? _____
c) Is he strong or weak? _____

Text C
a) What's the name of the man? _____
b) How old is Arnold? _____
c) How old is Arnold's mother? _____

LEARN THIS

How old are you?
A expressão **how old are you** é empregada para se perguntar a idade das pessoas.
A resposta pode ser dada por extenso:
I am sixteen years old. (Eu tenho 16 anos de idade.)
Ou de uma maneira abreviada:
I am sixteen. (Eu tenho 16.)
Quando perguntamos em inglês a idade de alguém, não usamos o verbo ter, como em português, mas sim o verbo **to be**:
How old are you?
A resposta também é dada com o verbo ser ou estar:
I am forty years old. (Eu estou com 40 anos de idade.)

ACTIVITIES

1 Answer the questions, following the pattern.

a) **How old are you? (14)**

   I am fourteen years old.

   I am fourteen.

b) How old is she? (13)

   _____

   _____

c) How old is he? (44)

   _____

   _____

d) How old is John? (31)

   _____

   _____

2 Answer the questions about you.

a) What's your name?
_____

b) How old are you?
_____

c) Who is your best friend?
_____

d) How old is he?
_____

e) How old are they?
_____

3 Add the numbers:

a) 42 + 12 = 54
   Forty-two plus twelve is fifty-four.

b) 24 + 62 =
_____

c) 37 + 25 =
_____

d) 60 + 30 =
_____

ROLE-PLAY – ORAL DRILL

Chame um colega à frente da classe e pergunte, em inglês, a idade dele e dos familiares. Segue uma sugestão:

(Chame seu colega)

Please come here!

– What's your name?
  – My name is… (O colega responde).
– Are you old or young?
  – I am… (O colega responde).
– How old are you?
  – I am…
– How old is your father?
  – My father is…
– How old is your mother?
  – My mother is…
– How old is your brother?
  – My brother is… or I have no brother.
– And how old is your sister?
  – My sister is… or I have no sister.

Word bank

come here: venha aqui
no: nenhum, nenhuma

Lesson 14

GENITIVE CASE

John's family

This is my family. There are four people in my family.
It is a happy family. I am the father. My name is John. I am forty years old.
Jane, my wife, is twenty-nine. She is a nice woman.
James, my first child, is ten years old. He is strong and intelligent.
Rose is my second child. She is a very pretty girl. She is six years old.
The dog in the picture is Toby. It is Rose's dog.
I love my wife and children very much.

TEXT COMPREHENSION

1 Answer the questions about the text:
a) **How many people are there in John's family?**
   There are four people.
b) Who is introducing his family?
   _____
c) What's the father's name?
   _____
d) How old is he?
   _____
e) What's the name of his wife?
   _____
f) How old is she?
   _____
g) What's the boy's name?
   _____
h) What's the girl's name?
   _____
i) What's the name of the dog?
   _____
j) Is John's family a happy family?
   _____

2 Write true (**T**) or false (**F**) according to the text:
a) **There are three people in John's family.** (**F**)
b) Jane is John's wife. ( )
c) Rose is a pretty girl. ( )
d) James is not strong. ( )
e) Rose and James are children. ( )
f) John loves his family. ( )

> **Word bank**
> **father's name:** nome do pai
> **boy's name:** nome do menino
> **John's wife:** esposa de John
> **children:** crianças, filhos

3 Connect according to the text:

a nice woman

a pretty girl

a happy man

a beautiful dog

an intelligent boy

LEARN THIS

Possessive case (**genitive case**)

Observe:

John's family (A família de John.)

O inglês, ao contrário do português, menciona em primeiro lugar a pessoa do possuidor e depois a posse.

Em vez da preposição **of** (de), usa-se apóstrofo seguido de **s** (**'s**) ou simplesmente apóstrofo (**'**) se o nome do possuidor já terminar por **s**:

James' father (O pai de James.)

Look at Sara's family

(My grandparents)

Shirley (my grandmother) + Samuel (my grandfather)

(My grandparents)

Daisy (my grandmother) + Donald (my grandfather)

(MY PARENTS)

Ralph (my father) + Jessica (my mother)   George (my uncle)   Susan (my aunt) + Mike (my uncle)

Mark (my brother)   Sara (me)   Chris (my sister)   Jack (my cousin)   Dora (my cousin)

eighty-three **83**

ACTIVITIES

1 Look at the pictures of Sara's family and answer the questions.

Who is...
a) Sara's sister? _____
b) Sara's brother? _____
c) Sara's father? _____
d) Sara's mother? _____
e) Sara's aunt? _____

Who are...
a) Sara's parents? _____
b) Sara's cousins? _____
c) Sara's uncles? _____
d) Sara's grandparents? _____

2 Answer according to Sara's family:

a) Who are Sara's parents?
_____

b) Who's Sara's aunt?
_____

c) Who are Sara's uncles?
_____

d) Who are Sara's cousins?
_____

3 In the space below draw your family tree.

My family tree

4 Answer the questions about your family.

a) Who are you? _____

b) Who are your grandparents? _____

c) What is your father's name? _____

d) What is your mother's name? _____

> **Observações**
>
> Com nome de pessoa que termina com **s,** é facultativo colocar **'s (Charles's)**.
>
> Quando o possuidor (no plural) terminar por **s (boys)**, não se usa apóstrofo mais **s ('s)**, e sim apenas um apóstrofo (**boys'**).
>
> Não se usa (**'s**) ou (**'**) com relação a coisas: ~~The table's legs.~~
>
> e sim **of the** (do, da, dos, das): **The legs of the table.** (As pernas da mesa.)

5 Write sentences in the genitive case:

a) Jane – flower – red
   Jane's flower is red.

b) Sandra – flower – yellow
   _____

6 Make sentences using the genitive case:

a) This – family – John
   This is John's family.

b) That – bike – Bob
   _____

c) This – farm – Donald
   _____

d) This – dress – Mary
   _____

7 Write in the genitive case using only the apostrophe (**'**):

a) house – Charles _____

b) dolls – Doris _____

c) farm – Louis _____

d) books – the pupils _____

e) bedroom – boys _____

f) girls – bikes _____

coisa possuída → **car**

possuidor → **James**

James' car

8 Write in English:

a) As pernas da cadeira. _____

b) A cor do carro. _____

c) As carteiras da escola. _____

d) Os galhos da árvore. _____

FUN TIME

Captain Ted's treasure

Captain Ted is going to the bottom of the sea for the first time. He wants to find a lost treasure under the deep water of the sea. Take a pencil and show him the way to the treasure.

ROLE-PLAY – ORAL DRILL

You and two classmates can dramatize the dialogue in front of the class.

A girl plays Betty's mother.

Another girl plays Betty's friend.

You play Betty. (You are Betty.)

Betty's house

- Mother, this is Monica, my classmate.
- Welcome to our house, Monica.
- Let me show you our house.
- This is John's bedroom.
- Oh, it's very large!
- It's very good.
- And this is my parents' bedroom.

— These are my mother's pictures.
— Oh!
— She paints very well!
— This is Meg's bedroom.
— And those are Meg's dolls. She likes dolls.
— This is my mother's garden. She likes flowers very much.
— Oh, you have a very beautiful house!

Lesson 15

COLORS

A picture in many colors

There are many colors in this picture.

The lake is blue. The sky is blue, too. The trees are green. The flowers are red and yellow. The little house is pink. The door of the little house is brown. There is a black cow in the picture.

There are white horses near the lake. There are black hens near the house.

And the children? Are they clean? Oh, no! They're not. They're dirty.

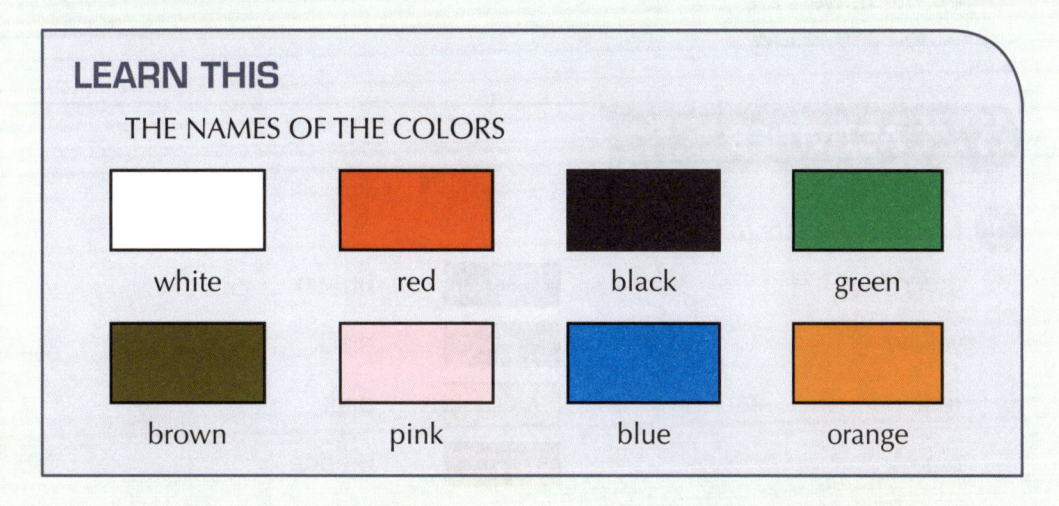

LEARN THIS

THE NAMES OF THE COLORS

white	red	black	green
brown	pink	blue	orange

TEXT COMPREHENSION

1 Match the columns according to the text:

1 blue   ○ sky
2 red   ○ hens
3 yellow   ○ cow
                ○ flower
4 black   ○ trees
5 green   ○ flower
                ○ door
6 white   ○ horses
7 pink   ○ lake
8 brown   ○ house

2 Write (F) for false or (T) for true according to the text and the picture:

a) The children are clean. ( )
b) The cow is white. ( )
c) The horses are white. ( )
d) The lake is white. ( )
e) The flowers are red and yellow. ( )

3 Answer according to the text and the picture:

a) **Are there many colors in the picture?**
   Yes, there are.

b) The house has many colors:
   What color is the door?
   _____
   What color are the walls?
   _____
   What color is the roof?
   _____

c) What color are the hens and the cow?
   _____

d) What color is the sky?
   _____

e) Are the horses white?
   _____

f) Are there red and yellow flowers in the picture?
   _____

g) What color is the girl's hat?
   _____

h) Are the boy's boots black?
   _____

i) Is the boy's bucket red?
   _____

ACTIVITIES

1 Match the colors to the words:

green   brown
yellow   black
red   pink
blue   orange

90 **ninety**

2 Write in English:

a) A flor é azul? Não, ela é vermelha.
_____
_____

b) A casa é verde? Não, ela é amarela.
_____
_____

c) O passarinho é verde? Sim, ele é verde.
_____
_____

d) Os livros são brancos? Não, eles são azuis.
_____
_____

3 Look at the example and answer the questions.

What color is:

a) the sunflower?

The sunflower is yellow. It is yellow.

b) the grass?
_____

c) milk?
_____

d) snow?
_____

e) coal?
_____

f) Sun?
_____

g) blood?
_____

4 Complete with colors:

a) A person may have:

_____ eyes, _____ eyes, _____ eyes, _____ eyes.

b) What's the color of your eyes?

My eyes are _____.

c) A person may have:

_____ hair, _____ hair, _____ hair.

d) What color is your hair?

_____.

ninety-one 91

FUN TIME

1 Color the picture:

The house = red
The trees = green and brown
The birds = blue
The horse = brown

The cow = black
The boy = many colors
The dog = brown
The cat = white

2 Color the seasons:

blue ⟶ winter
green ⟶ spring
red ⟶ summer
yellow ⟶ autumn or fall

Summer

Winter

Spring

Autumn

92 ninety-two

3 Write the colors of the flags:

Brazilian flag

a) **The Brazilian flag is: green, yellow, blue and white.**

German flag

e) _____

Japanese flag

b) _____

Canadian flag

f) _____

Turkish flag

c) _____

American flag

g) _____

Nigerian flag

d) _____

English flag

h) _____

ROLE-PLAY – ORAL DRILL

A classe pode organizar uma atividade sobre as cores em inglês.

Sob a coordenação do professor, os alunos perguntam uns aos outros, mostrando coisas coloridas que estejam na sala. Fala-se o nome do colega e se faz a pergunta. Ele deve responder também em inglês.

Segue sugestão de perguntas e respostas:

– (Fale o nome do(a) colega), **what color is this pencil?**
– **It is...** (**That pencil is...**)
– (Nome do(a) colega), **what color is the table of the class?**
– **The table is...** (**It is...**)
– (Nome do(a) colega), **is this pen blue?**
– **Yes, it is.** (**No, it is not. It is...**)
– (Nome do(a) colega), **are these papers white?**
– **Yes, they are.** (**No, they are not white. They are...**)
– (Nome do(a) colega), **is my hair black or blond?**
– **Your hair is...**
– (Nome do(a) colega), **what color is my shirt... my blouse...**
– (Nome do(a) colega), **what color are my shoes... my tennis shoes...**

ninety-three

Lesson 16

POSSESSIVE ADJECTIVES: HIS, HER, THEIR

A guessing game

Can you guess the color of his hair? What is the color of his eyes?

No! His eyes are not brown and his hair is not blond.

Yes! I can guess! His eyes are brown and his hair is blond.

His hair is black and his eyes are green.

Oh, no! You are wrong!

His eyes are black and his hair is black, too.

Oh, very good! You are right! You won a CD.

What color is her hair?

What color are her eyes?

And now... Can you guess the color of her hair? What is the color of her eyes?

GUESSING GAME

Yes! I can guess! Her eyes are brown and her hair is black.

No! Her eyes are not brown and her hair is not black.

Her hair is brown and her eyes are black.

Oh, no! You are wrong!

Her eyes are blue and her hair is blond.

Oh, very good! You are right! You win a roller skate.

ninety-five 95

TEXT COMPREHENSION

1 Complete the box according to the text.

What is the color of

the boy's hair?	the boy's eyes?
the girl's hair?	the girl's eyes?

2 Answer the questions according to the text:

Observação: As perguntas com o possessivo **his** referem-se ao menino e as perguntas com **her** referem-se à menina.

a) What color are his eyes?

_____

b) What color are her eyes?

_____

c) Are his eyes brown?

_____

d) Are her eyes black?

e) Is his hair blond?

_____

f) Is her hair blond?

_____

g) Is her hair black?

_____

LEARN THIS

1. Veja as duas maneiras de perguntar sobre cores:
   a) **What is the color of your hair?**
   b) **What color is the book?** (singular)
   What color are the books? (plural)

2. Possessive: his – her
   His significa dele, seu, sua. Refere-se sempre a uma pessoa do sexo masculino.
   George lives in a house. His house is beautiful.
   (George mora numa casa. Sua casa é bonita.)
   Her significa dela, sua, seu. Refere-se sempre a uma pessoa do sexo feminino.
   Mary lives in a flat. Her flat is beautiful.
   (Mary mora num apartamento. Seu apartamento é bonito.)
   A forma plural de **his** e **her** é **their**.
   Their significa deles, delas, seus, suas.
   Their refere-se tanto a pessoas de ambos os sexos como a animais e coisas.
   Jane and John live in a house. Their house is modern.
   (Jane e John vivem numa casa. A casa deles é moderna.)

ACTIVITIES

1 Complete the sentences with his or her:

a) Chris has got a book. _____ book is very interesting.

b) My teacher Mary has got a red car. _____ car is old.

c) Paul, my father, has got a red car, too. _____ car is new.

d) Look! Jane is going out with _____ father.

e) Look! Fred is going out with _____ mother.

f) My father is reading _____ newspaper.

g) Mary is studying _____ lesson.

h) Chris is dancing with _____ friend.

i) What is her name? _____ name is Dolores.

j) What is his name? _____ name is Edson.

2 Write in the plural:

a) His house is modern. _____

b) Her friend is playing basketball. _____

c) His books are in the bag. _____

REVIEW

1 Observe the dialogue below:

Sam: Who is the boy in the picture?
Julie: He is my friend John.
Sam: How old is he?
Julie: He is about twenty years old.
Sam: Is he tall or short?
Julie: He is tall.
Sam: What color are his eyes?
Julie: His eyes are black.
Sam: What color is his hair?
Julie: His hair is black, too.
Sam: What color are the boy's trousers?
Julie: They are black.
Sam: What color is his T-shirt?
Julie: It is white.

2 And now it's your turn.

Complete the dialogue:

A friend: Who is the girl in the picture? (Mary)
You: _____

A friend: How old is she? (15)
You: _____

A friend: Is Mary tall or short?
You: _____

A friend: What color are her eyes?
You: _____

A friend: What color is her hair?
You: _____

A friend: What color is Mary's blouse?
You: _____

A friend: What color are Mary's trousers/pants?
You: _____

3 Answer these questions about you:

a) What's your name?
_____

b) How old are you?
_____

c) Are you short or tall?
_____

d) What color are your eyes?
_____

e) What color is your hair?
_____

f) What color is your shirt?
_____

g) What color are your trousers?
_____

4 Look at the pictures and write the colors:

What color is this rose?
_____

What color is this sunflower?
_____

98   ninety-eight

Lesson 7

VERBS GO, DO, WATCH: PREPOSITIONS OF TIME

Jessica's daily routine

1. Jessica gets up at seven o'clock every day.

2. She has breakfast at seven-thirty.

3. At eight o'clock she goes to school.

4. At twelve o'clock she comes back home.

5. She has lunch at one o'clock p.m.

6. From two to four o'clock Jessica does her homework.

7. From four to six she plays
– with her friends.

8. Jessica has her dinner at
– seven-thirty p.m.

9. At eight o'clock she
– watches TV with her parents.

10. At ten o'clock she goes to
– bed to sleep.

TEXT COMPREHENSION

1 Complete Jessica's timetable according to the text.

a) Jessica gets up at _____.

b) Her breakfast is at _____.

c) She goes to school at _____.

d) Her lunch is at _____.

e) She does her homework from _____ to _____.

f) She plays from _____ to _____.

g) She has dinner at _____.

h) She goes to bed at _____.

2 And now it's your turn.

Complete your timetable.

a) I get up at _____

b) I have breakfast at _____

c) I go to school at _____

d) I have lunch at _____

e) I do my homework from _____ to _____

f) I play from _____ to _____

g) I have dinner at _____

h) I watch TV from _____ to _____

i) I go to bed at _____

3 Answer the question.

What are the meals of the day?

_____

_____

_____

_____

_____

LEARN THIS

Observe como dizemos as horas em inglês:

What time is it? What's the time? (Que horas são?)

It's five o'clock. (São cinco horas.)

It's midday. (É meio-dia.)

It's midnight. (É meia-noite.)

- Quando dizemos as horas exatas (sem os minutos), acrescentamos a expressão **o'clock**.
  (As horas e os minutos você estudará na próxima lição.)

- Quando queremos indicar que se trata de horas antes ou depois do meio-dia, usamos as expressões **ante meridian** (antes do meio-dia) e **post meridian** (depois do meio-dia) que são abreviadas **a.m.** e **p.m.** Observe:

  It's seven a.m. (São sete da manhã.)

  It's five p.m. (São cinco da tarde.)

- Há, também, outra maneira de perguntar as horas:

  What's the time? (Que horas são?)

- Na expressão **o'clock** este **o'** é a contração de **of the**:

  It's five o'clock = It is five of the clock.

ACTIVITIES

1 Make the question and then answer it:

a) **What time is it?**

   It's six o'clock.

b) What time is it?
   _____

c) What time is it?
   _____

d) What time is it?
   _____

102 one hundred and two

Lesson 18
Telling the time; Days of the week

What's the time?

Jenny: Excuse me. What's the time, please?
Can you tell me?
Max: Sure. It's exactly five o'clock.
Jenny: Thank you very much.
I want to take the bus number 21.
Max: The bus number 21 stops here.
Jenny: Thank you.
Max: You're welcome.

TEXT COMPREHENSION

1 Answer according to the text:

a) Who asks the time? _____

b) Are Jenny and Max at home or in the street? _____

c) Who has a watch: Jenny or Max? _____

d) What's the number of the bus that Jenny wants to take? _____

e) Draw a traffic sign Bus Stop:

Alice's party

Sara: Mom, I think we are late.
Carol: What time is Alice's party?
Sara: At seven-thirty.
Carol: And what time is it now?
Sara: It's ten to eight.
Carol: Oh, my God! We are late.
Sara: Hurry up! Let's go.

TEXT COMPREHENSION

1 Who is the daughter in the dialogue? _____

2 Who is the mother? _____

3 What time is Alice's party? _____

4 Are Sara and Carol in time for Alice's party or are they late? _____

5 How many minutes are Sara and Carol late for Alice's party? _____

LEARN THIS

ABOUT TIME

Months
Weeks
Days
Hours
Minutes
Seconds

There are twelve months in a year.
There are seven days in a week.
There are twenty-four hours in a day.
There are sixty minutes in an hour.
There are sixty seconds in a minute.

DAYS OF THE WEEK

The days of the week are:
Sunday Monday Tuesday Wednesday Thursday Friday Saturday

This is a clock.   This is an alarm clock.   This is a watch.

1. **The minute hand is on the right side of the clock.**
(O ponteiro dos minutos está no lado direito do relógio.)

WHAT TIME IS IT?

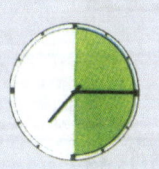

7:05
It's five past seven.
It's seven five.

7:10
It's ten past seven.
It's seven ten.

7:15
It's a quarter past seven.
It's seven fifteen.

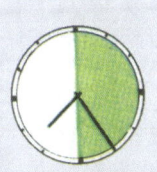

7:25
It's twenty-five past seven.
It's seven twenty-five.

7:30
It's half past seven.
It's seven-thirty.

2. **The minute hand is on the left side of the clock.**
(O ponteiro dos minutos está no lado esquerdo do relógio.)

7:35
It's twenty-five to eight.
It's seven thirty-five.

7:40
It's twenty to eight.
It's seven forty.

7:45
It's a quarter to eight.
It's seven forty-five.

7:55
It's five to eight.
It's seven fifty-five.

ACTIVITIES

1 What time is it?

6:00 — It's six o'clock.

6:35 — It's twenty-five to seven.

6:05 — _____

6:40 — _____

6:10 — _____

6:45 — _____

6:15 — _____

6:50 — _____

6:20 — _____

6:55 — _____

`6:25` _____

`10:00` _____

`6:30` _____

`10:40` _____

2 Choose the correct alternative:

a) `2:10`
( ) It's ten to two.
( ) It's ten past two.

c) `4:15`
( ) It's fifteen to four.
( ) It's fifteen past four.

b) `1:58`
( ) It's fifty-eight to one.
( ) It's fifty-eight past two.
( ) It's two to two.

d) `11:05`
( ) It's five past eleven.
( ) It's five to twelve.

ROLE-PLAY – ORAL DRILL

A classe pode organizar uma atividade sobre as horas em inglês. Sob a coordenação do professor, os alunos sorteados perguntam aos colegas as horas, em inglês, movimentando os ponteiros de um grande relógio de cartolina, previamente preparado.

Segue sugestão de perguntas e respostas:

Um(a) aluno(a) pergunta para o(a)colega: **What time is it?**

O(a) colega responde: **It is...**

O(a) aluno(a) pergunta novamente: **Is it ten o'clock?**

O(a) colega responde conforme a hora real: **Yes, it is. No, it is not. It is...**

O(a) aluno(a) pergunta outra vez: **Is it half past seven?**

O(a) colega responde conforme a hora real: **Yes, it is. No, it is not. It is...**

Lesson 19
SIMPLE PRESENT OF VERB TO HAVE

A penpal

Bridge of Weir School
Warlock Road,
Bridge of Weir – Scotland
PB12 309
22nd. December 2010

Dear friend, Robert

I am ten years old and my name is Joanne Simpson. My best friends are Chris, Max and Jessica. I sit next to Chris in class.

On Mondays I play volleyball at the club.

My teacher is Mrs Ellis. My school starts at ten past nine and finishes at half past three.

I have black hair and black eyes.

I have a brother named Paul and a sister named Sara. My brother is eleven and my sister is thirteen.

I wish you a Merry Christmas and a Happy New Year.

From your penpal,

Joanne.

Here's a photo of me.

TEXT COMPREHENSION

1 Answer the questions:

a) What country is Joanne from?
_____

b) What's the penpal's name?
_____

c) How old is Joanne?
_____

d) What are Joanne's best friends?
_____

e) Who sits beside Joanne in the class?
_____

f) Who is Joanne's teacher?
_____

g) What is Joanne like? (Como é a Joana?)
_____

h) What's her brother's name?
_____

i) What's her sister's name?
_____

j) How old is her brother?
_____

k) How old is her sister?
_____

LEARN THIS

IMPORTANT EXPRESSIONS IN CONVERSATION

Thanks: Obrigado

Thank you: Obrigado

I'm well/I'm fine: Estou bem

I'm very well: Estou muito bem

I'm OK: Estou bem

I'm sick: Estou mal, estou doente

I'm not well: Não estou bem

I'm sorry: Sinto muito

What's the matter?: Qual é o problema?

What's the problem?: Qual é o problema?

What's the trouble?: Qual é o problema?

Not at all: De nada, não há de quê

Congratulations!: Parabéns!

So long: Até logo

Over there: Lá, ali, acolá

Please: Por favor

Excuse me: Desculpe-me, com licença

Nice to meet you: Prazer em conhecê-lo(la)

Glad to meet you: Prazer em conhecê-lo(la)

It's a pleasure to meet you: Prazer em conhecê-lo(la)

You're welcome: A seu dispor, de nada, não há de quê

Don't disturb: Não perturbe

Keep silence: Silêncio!

Don't worry!: Não se preocupe!

No problem!: Sem problemas!

one hundred and nine **109**

LET'S SING

Silent night!

Silent night! Silent night!
Holy night!
All is calm. All is bright,
'round yon virgin Mother and Child.
Holy infant so tender and mild,
Sleep in heavenly peace,
Sleep in heavenly peace.

Word bank
silent: silencioso, quieto
holy: santo, sagrado
bright: brilhante, luminoso
'round (around): em volta, em torno
yon: lá, aquele, aquela (forma antiga de yonder: lá, acolá)
tender: tenro, delicado
mild: meigo
heavenly: celestial
peace: paz

Additional texts

Water

Water is the principal surce of life on Earth.
Man uses water for many purposes. Look:
Fish need water to live.
Plants need water to grow.
People drink water to live.
Nobody lives without water.
People use water to wash and clean things.
We take a shower.
We use water to take a bath.
Man uses water to produce energy.
Waterfalls attract tourists.
We use water to relax.
Animals need water to live.

> **Word bank**
>
> **shower:** banho de chuveiro
> **bath:** banho de banheira, de mar, de rio, lago...

TEXT COMPREHENSION

1 Write sentences according to the pictures:

_____   _____
_____   _____

Water is a very limited resource, so:

Save Water!
Don't Waste it!
Don't pollute it!

ACTIVITIES

1 Complete:

We use water to _____

We use water _____

We use water _____

People use water to _____

Animals _____

2 Translate:

Plants need water to grow.
_____

We use water to quench the thirst and to wash things.
_____

LISTEN AND WRITE – DICTATION

_____
_____
_____
_____
_____

At the zoo

Julie: Look, dad! Those monkeys in that tree! How funny they are!
Dad: Yes, they are funny
Julie: Can I give these bananas to that one? The black one? He wants these bananas!
Dad: You can't give the bananas, Julie. It is forbbiden to give food to the animals in the zoo.
Julie: He is making grimaces. He is very funny!

TEXT COMPREHENSION

1 Where are Julie and dad?
_____

2 Where are the monkeys?
_____

3 Monkeys are
( ) lazy   ( ) funny   ( ) angry

4 Monkeys like to eat
( ) carrots   ( ) bananas   ( ) oranges

5 Who wants bananas?

( ) Julie   ( ) dad   ( ) the black monkey

6 What is forbbiden in the zoo?

( ) give food to the animals   ( ) eat bananas   ( ) shoot pictures

7 Are the monkeys near or far from Julie?

_____

My school

I study in a very good school.

The name of my school is Thomas Edison School. It is not large but it's very nice and clean.

There are many boys and girls in my school. There are many teachers, too. All the teachers are good. Some teachers are young but others are elderly.

There is only one principal. He is a very serious man.

I like my school. I am very happy in my school.

TEXT COMPREHENSION

1 Questions on the text:

a) What is the name of the school? _____

b) Is it a good school? _____

c) Is it large or small? _____

d) Is it dirty or clean? _____

e) Who is a very serious man? _____

f) How many principals are there in the school? _____

2 Underline the words that refer to school:

Book	Eraser	Cow	Classmate
Pencil	Lake	Student	Ink
Stove	Sky	Chalk	Ship
Copybook	Teacher	Student	Desk
Ruler	Principal	Train	Map
Refrigerator	Bird	Classroom	Beach

Silvia introduces her family

This is my family.
There are six people in my family.
We are at home now. The house is not beautiful but it is large and clean. We are very happy in this house.

This is my father.
His name is John.
He is sixty-five years old.
His hair is already white.
His eyes are brown.

These are my children.
This is my son Mark.
He is only 10 years old.
His hair is blond.
His eyes are blue.

This is my mother.
Her name is Flavia.
She is fifty-five.
Her hair is blond.
Her eyes are blue.

And this is my daughter Mary.
She is fourteen years old.
Her hair is blond and her eyes are green.

This is my husband.
I am his wife.
His name is Paul.
He is forty years old.
His hair is black and his eyes are green.

This is me.
I am Silvia.
I am thirty-two.
My hair is brown and my eyes are blue.

TEXT COMPREHENSION

1 Answer the questions about the characters of the text:

a) Who introduces her family?
_____

b) Is John young or old?
_____

c) How old is he?
_____

d) What color are his eyes?
_____

e) How old is Flavia?
_____

f) What color are her eyes?
_____

g) What color is her hair?
_____

The blind man and the guide

— Are there cars in the street?
— No, there are no cars in the street.

— Are there holes in the ground?
— No, there are not!

— I am hungry. Is there a snack bar nearby?
— No, there is not!

— Are there dogs in the house?
— No, there are no dogs in the house.

— Is there a bird in the tree?
— Yes. There is.

— Is there a taxi for me?
— No, there are no taxis in the street.

— Then, let's walk...

General vocabulary

A

a (an): um, uma
abandon: abandonar
about: sobre, aproximadamente, a respeito de
above: acima
according to: de acordo com
actor: ator
actress: atriz
add: acrescentar
address: endereço
admit: admitir
advice: conselho
age: idade
afternoon: tarde
airplane (plane): avião
all: tudo, todo, toda
alone: sozinho
along: ao longo de, ao lado
already: já
am: sou, estou
and so on: e assim por diante
another: outro(a)
answer: resposta, responder
ant: formiga
any: algum, nenhum
anything: alguma coisa; nada
anything else: algo mais
apple: maçã

appointment: encontro
are: somos, estamos...
are there...?: há...? (plural)
around: em volta
ask: perguntar, pedir
at: em, a
at home: em casa
attract: atrair
at the beach: na praia
aunt: tia
autumn: outono

B

baby: bebê
bad: mau
bag: mala
bald: careca
ball: bola
ball pen: esferográfica
balloon: balão
bargain: barganha
bass: baixo (instrumento)
bath: banho de banheira, de mar, de rio
be: ser, estar
beach: praia
beautiful: bonito(a)
because: porque
bed: cama

bedroom: quarto de dormir
bee: abelha
begin: começar, começam
below: debaixo, abaixo
beside: ao lado de
best: melhor
between: entre
big: grande
bird: pássaro
birth: nascimento
black: preto(a)
blind: cego(a)
blond (blonde): loiro(a)
blood: sangue
blouse: blusa
blue: azul
boat: barco
book: livro
bookshop: livraria
boot: bota
bottom: fundo
boy: menino, rapaz
box: caixa, quadro
Brazilian: brasileiro(a)
bread: pão
breakfast: café da manhã
bright: iluminado, brilhante
brother: irmão
brown: marrom
bucket: balde
bull: touro
bus: ônibus
but: mas
butter: manteiga
butterfly: borboleta

buy: comprar
by: por, de
bye: até logo

C

call: chamar
called: chamado
calm: calmo(a)
CD: compact disk, disco compacto
can: posso, pode...
car: carro
car racer: piloto de corrida
carrot: cenoura
cartoon: desenho em quadrinhos
cat: gato(a)
cell phone: celular
chair: cadeira
chalk: giz
change: mudar, trocar; troco
cheap: barato(a)
child: criança
children: crianças; filhos(as)
choose: escolher
class: classe
classmate: colega de classe
classroom: sala de aula
clean: limpar, limpo
climb: subir
close (verb): fechar
close (prep.): próximo, perto
clothes: roupas
coal: carvão
color: pintar, pinte
come: vir
come back: voltar, volte, volto

come in: entrar, entre...
congratulations: parabéns
copybook: caderno
cost: custar
could: podia...
country: país
cousin: primo, prima
cow: vaca
cowboy: vaqueiro, peão de fazenda
crazy: doido(a), maluco(a)
cross: cruzar; cruz
cry: chorar; gritar
cupboard: armário de cozinha
customer: freguês, freguesa

D
dad: pai
dark: escuro
daughter: filha
daughter's head: cabeça da filha
day: dia
deaf: surdo(a)
dear: querido(a)
deep: profundo(a)
desk: carteira
dial: discar
dinner: jantar
dirty: sujo(a)
disappear: desaparecer
divide: dividir
divided: dividido
do: fazer, faça...
does: faz
don't: não
door: porta

doctor: médico
doctor's: consultório médico
dog: cachorro
doll: boneca
dot to dot: ponto a ponto
dotted: pontilhado(a)
double: dobrar
downtown: centro da cidade
draw: desenhar
drawer: gaveta
dress: vestido
drill: exercício, treino
drink: beber
drive: dirigir
duck: pato
dumb: mudo(a)

E
each: cada
each other: um ao outro
ear: orelha; ouvido
earth: terra
easy: fácil
eat: comer
egg: ovo
empty: vazio(a)
end: fim
energy: energia
English: inglês
enter: entrar
entrance: entrada
eraser: borracha
evening: noite, anoitecer
every: cada
everybody: todos(as)

exactly: exatamente
excuse me: desculpe-me
expensive: caro(a)
explain: explicar
eyes: olhos

F
fall: cair, caem
family: família
family tree: árvore genealógica
far: longe
farm: fazenda
fast: rápido(a)
fat: gordo(a)
father: pai
father's name: nome do pai
fifth: quinto, quinta
find: encontrar
fine: bem, bom, ótimo
finger: dedo
finish: terminar, acabar
fire: fogo
fireman: bombeiro
firefighter: bombeiro
first: primeiro
first time: primeira vez
fish: peixe
fit: assentar, combinar
flag: bandeira
flat: apartamento
flower: flor
fly: voar
follow: seguir, siga
food: alimento, comida
for: para

forest: floresta
fountain: fonte
Friday: sexta-feira
friend: amigo(a)
from: de (origem)
full: cheio
fun: divertimento
fun time: hora de diversão
funny: engraçado, divertido

G
game: jogo
garden: jardim
genitive case: caso genitivo
get: conseguir, ter, adquirir
get up: levantar
get off: sair, descer de veículo
ghost: fantasma
girl: menina, garota, moça
girl's name: nome da menina
give: dar, dê...
glass: copo
glasses: óculos, copos
go: ir, vá, vou...
goalkeeper: goleiro(a)
God: Deus
goes: vai
going to: indo para
gold: ouro
good: bom, boa
good afternoon: boa tarde
good morning: bom dia
go out: sair
grade: grau, série
grandfather: avô

grandmother: avó
grandson: neto
grass: grama, relva
green: verde
greeting: cumprimento, saudação
grey: cinzento(a)
grimace: careta
ground: chão
grow: crescer, cultivar
guess: adivinhar, adivinhe...
gymnastic athlete: atleta de ginástica

H

hair: cabelo
half: metade, meio
hand: mão
handsome: bonito, elegante (usa-se só para os homens)
happen: acontecer
happy: feliz
has, has got: tem
hat: chapéu
have: ter, tenho
head: cabeça
headache: dor de cabeça
hear: escutar
heaven: céu
heavenly: celeste, divino
help: ajudar; socorro
hen: galinha
her: dela
here: aqui
here you are: aqui estão
hill: colina
his: dele, seu...
hobby: passatempo

hole: buraco
holy: santo, sagrado
home: casa, lar
homework: trabalho de casa, lição de casa
horse: cavalo
hot: quente
hour: hora
house: casa
how: como
How are you?: Como vai você?
how many: quantos(as)
how much: quanto
How old are you?: Qual é sua idade?
hungry: com fome, faminto(a)
hurry up: apressar-se
husband: marido

I

I: eu
ill: doente
I'm: eu sou, eu estou
I'm fine: eu estou bem
I'm very well: eu estou muito bem
in: em
in a: em um, em uma
indeed: de fato, realmente
ink: tinta
infant: criança, bebê
interesting: interessante
in this: neste, nesta
in time: dentro do horário
introduce: apresentar
invite: convidar
is: é, está
is there?: há? (singular)

it: ele, ela
it's: ele é, está; ela é, está
it's not = it isn't: não é, não está
I've got: eu tenho...

J

job: trabalho, emprego
just: apenas

K

keep: guardar, conservar
key: chave; tecla
kite: pipa
know: conhecer, saber

L

lake: lago
lamp: lâmpada
large: espaçoso(a), grande
last name: sobrenome
late: atrasado(a)
lazy: preguiçoso(a)
leaf: folha
learn: aprender, aprenda
leave: deixar, partir
leaves: folhas
left: esquerda (deixou, partiu)
leg: perna
lesson: lição, aula
let me: deixe-me
let's: vamos
let's go: vamos
let's sing: vamos cantar
letter: carta
life: vida

like: gostar
like: como
lion: leão
listen: escutar, escute
little: pequeno(a), pouco
live: morar, viver
look: olhar, olhe...
look at: olhar para
look for: procurar, procure...
look like: parecer
lost: perdido(a)
love: amar, amor
lovely: amável, adorável
lunch: almoço; lanche
lunch time: hora do almoço

M

magazine: revista
make: fazer, fabricar
man: homem
many: muitos(as)
map: mapa
match: unir, emparelhar, partida, fósforo
may: pode
meal: refeição
meet: encontrar, conhecer (pessoas)
mechanic: mecânico
medicine: rémedio
midday: meio-dia
middle: meio
mild: meigo, afável
milk: leite
minus: menos
mistake: erro

mom: mãe, mamãe
monkey: macaco
month: mês
Monday: segunda-feira
moon: lua
morning: manhã
mother: mãe
mouse: rato
mouth: boca
much: muito
multiply: multiplicar
musician: músico
must: precisar, precisa...
my: meu, minha...
my teacher's name: o nome de meu (minha) professor (a)

N

name: nome
named: chamado(a)
near: perto
neck: pescoço
need: preciso, precisar
nervous: nervoso(a)
nest: ninho
new: novo
news: notícia, novidade
newspaper: jornal
next: próximo, seguinte
nice: bonito(a), bom, boa, bacana
nice to meet you: prazer em conhecê-lo(a)
night: noite
no: não; nenhum
nose: nariz
note: nota, anotar

now: agora
number: número
nurse: enfermeira

O

occupation: profissão, ocupação
ocean: oceano
of: de
office boy: mensageiro, auxiliar de escritório
of course: naturalmente
of the: do, da, dos, das
old: velho(a)
on: sobre, em, no, na...
one: um, uma
only: somente
on the left: à esquerda
on the right: à direita
open: abrir, abra
opposite: antônimo
or: ou
orange: laranja
order: ordem, encomendar
our: nosso

P

paint: pintar
painter: pintor(a)
pair: par
parents: pais
partner: colega, companheiro(a)
party: festa
past: depois, passado
pattern: modelo
peace: paz
pen: caneta

penpal: amigo(a) por correspondência
pencil: lápis
people: pessoas
person: pessoa
phone call: chamada telefônica
picture: figura, quadro, pintura
pilot: piloto(a)
pink: cor-de-rosa
pipe: cano
pillow: travesseiro
place: lugar
plant: planta, plantar
play: jogar, brincar; fazer o papel de, tocar instrumento
player: jogador(a)
pleasant: agradável
please: por favor
pleased: satisfeito(a)
plumber: encanador(a)
pocket: bolso
politician: político
pollute: poluir
poor: pobre
pretty: bonito(a)
price: preço
principal: diretor; principal
produce: produzir
protect: proteger
purpose: propósito, finalidade
purse: bolsa
puzzle: quebra-cabeça

Q
quench: saciar a sede
question: pergunta

R
rain: chuva
read: ler, leia...
red: vermelho(a)
redeemer: redentor(a)
refrigerator: geladeira
relax: relaxar
repair: consertar
resource: recurso
rewrite: reescrever
review: revisão
ride: cavalgar
rich: rico(a)
right: certo, direito
road: estrada
roar: urrar, rugir
role-play: encenação, representação
room: sala
round (around): em volta, em torno
rope: corda
ruler: régua
run: correr
runner: corredor(a)

S
same: mesmo(a)
Saturday: sábado
save: economizar
say: dizer, dizemos
school: escola
schoolbag: mala escolar, mochila
second: segundo
secretary: secretária
sea: mar
see: ver

seem: parecer
see you tomorrow: até amanhã
sell: vender
serious: sério(a)
she's: ela é, ela está
ship: navio
shirt: camisa
shoe: sapato
shop: loja
short: curto; baixo
shorts: calção, short
show: espetáculo; mostrar
shower: banho de chuveiro
shut: fechar
side: lado
silent: silêncioso, quieto
sing: cantar
singer: cantor(a)
sink: pia
sister: irmã
sit: sentar
situation: situação
skin: pele
skirt: saia
sky: céu
slacks: calças
sleep: dormir, durma
slow: vagaroso(a)
slowly: vagarosamente, devagar
slum: favela
small: pequeno(a)
smart: esperto(a), inteligente
smell: cheirar
smoke: fumar
snow: neve

so: tão; por isso
soccer: futebol
soccer player: jogador(a) de futebol
socks: meias (curtas)
stockings: meias (compridas)
so long: até logo
somebody: alguém
son: filho
song: canção
so that: de modo que
space: espaço
speak: falar
spring: primavera
square: quadrado
star: estrela
start: começar
statue: estátua
stop: parar, parada
story: história
stove: fogão
strange: estranho, esquisito(a)
string: linha, barbante
street: rua
strong: forte
student: estudante
study: estudar
summer: verão
sun: sol
Sunday: domingo
sunflower: girassol
sunny: ensolarado(a)
sure: certamente, claro, seguramente
surname: sobrenome
swim: nadar
swimmer: nadador(a)

T

table: mesa
tail: cauda, rabo
take: tomar, pegar, levar
take a bath: tomar banho (de banheira, piscina, mar)
take a shower: tomar banho (de chuveiro)
talk: conversar
tall: alto(a)
teacher: professor, professora
tell: contar, dizer
telling: contando, dizendo
tender: frágil, delicado
tennis shoes: tênis
terrible: terrível
thanks: obrigado(a)
thank you: obrigado(a)
that: aquele; que; aquilo
the: o, a, os, as
their: deles, delas
there: lá
there are: há (plural)
there is: há (singular)
these: estes, estas
they're: eles/elas são, estão
thin: magro, fino
thing: coisa
think: pensar
thirst: sede
this: este, esta, isto
this way: desse modo, dessa maneira
thrilling: excitante, emocionante, vibrante
Thursday: quinta-feira
ticket: bilhete, passagem
time: tempo
time (in time): a tempo, no horário
times: vezes
title: título
today: hoje
to: para, até
toad: sapo
tomorrow: amanhã
too: também; demais
touch: tocar
town: cidade
traffic sign: sinal de trânsito
train: trem
translate: traduzir, traduza
treasure: tesouro
tree: árvore
trouble: problema
trousers: calças
truck: caminhão
true: verdadeiro(a)
try: experimentar, tentar
tube: cano
Tuesday: terça-feira
turn off: desligar
turn on: ligar

U

ugly: feio(a)
uncle: tio
under: debaixo
underline: sublinhar
understand: entender, compreender
unhappy: infeliz
use: usar, uso

V

vacation: férias

vase: vaso

vegetables: legumes

very: muito

very much: muitíssimo

W

wait: esperar

walk: andar, caminhar

want: querer, desejar

wardrobe: armário

warm: quente

wash: lavar

waste: desperdiçar

water: água

waterfall: cachoeira

way: caminho

weak: fraco(a)

weather: tempo

Wednesday: quarta-feira

week: semana

we're: nós somos, estamos

welcome: bem-vindo

well: bem

what: o que, qual

What do you do?: O que você faz?

What's the weather like?: Como está o tempo?

what's: qual é, está

When: quando

where: onde

who: quem

Who are you?: Quem é você?

white: branco(a)

wife: esposa

with: com

win: ganhar, vencer

wind: vento

window: janela

winter: inverno

woman: mulher

won: ganhou

wonderful: maravilhoso(a)

word: palavra

word-hunt: caça-palavra

work: trabalhar, trabalho

worker: trabalhador, operário

write: escrever

writting papers: papéis para escrever

wrong: errado(a)

Y

year: ano

yellow: amarelo(a)

yes: sim

yet: ainda

you: você, vocês

young: jovem

you are: você é, você está...

you're welcome: de nada

your: seu, sua, seus, suas

Z

zoo: zoológico

zebra: zebra